CHURCH MEETINGS
THAT MATTER

PHILIP A. ANDERSON

CHURCH MEETINGS THAT MATTER

THE PILGRIM PRESS

New York

The scripture quotations in this publication are (unless otherwise indicated) from the *Revised Standard Version of the Bible,* copyrighted 1946 and 1952 by the Division of Christian Education, National Council of Churches, and are used by permission.

Library of Congress Cataloging-in-Publication Data

Anderson, Philip A., 1922–
    Church meetings that matter.

    Bibliography: p. 111.
    1. Church meetings.   2. Church group
work.   I. Title.
BV652.15.A5   1987   254′.6   86-30262
ISBN 0-8298-0752-7 (pbk.)

The Pilgrim Press, 132 West 31 Street, New York, New York 10001

CONTENTS

78963

I

GOING
TO A MEETING

I'm tired of going to church meetings that really don't matter." Almost all Christians, ministers and laymen alike, have expressed this frustration at one time or another. Active church members spend many hours each month in various kinds of church meetings, too many of which, on reflection, appear to have been a waste of time.

Why is this so? Who is responsible? And what can be done about it? Much is known about what happens in meetings, and how, and why. There is more to a good meeting than having a "good" chairman and a mimeographed agenda.

It is the purpose of this book to help readers understand what this "more" is, what goes on in small group meetings at the church, how meetings can make a difference in our lives, and what we can do to bring about *church meetings that matter.*

It is the thesis of this book that *leaders* of church meetings, both clergy and laity, can nurture the growth and increase the participation of the members of their groups and that *members* of church meetings can influence the efficiency and productivity of the meetings they attend. All are responsible. If a meeting is poor, rarely is it entirely the leader's fault. It is more likely that other persons in the meeting have failed their responsibilities too.

Meetings in the church promise new relationships in which life is based not upon status and prestige but upon love for one another. In the church, persons are to be known as they really are, participating in a community of honesty, integrity, trust, forgiveness, reconciliation, and mercy. Such community is the experience recorded in the Bible and in the history of the church and preached about in the churches today. Too often this community never comes into being. Problems arise in our congregations and in our meetings. Members become reluctant participants; they tolerate, avoid, or try to manipulate the others. Sadly, the life we live is cold, calculating, nonaccepting, a denial of the life we profess.

It does not have to be this way. Meetings in the church can and should allow us to make the same affirmation Paul made in Ephesians 2:19-22: "So you are no longer outsiders or aliens, but fellow citizens with every other Christian—you belong now to the household of God. Firmly beneath you is the foundation, God's messengers and prophets, the actual foundationstone being Christ Jesus himself. In him each separate piece of building, properly fitting into its neighbor, grows together into a temple consecrated to the Lord. You are all part of this building in which God himself lives by his Spirit"—*The New Testament in Modern English,* trans. J. B. Phillips (New York: Macmillan, 1962).

THREE TYPES OF MEETINGS IN THE CHURCH

Almost every time a person sets foot in his church, he meets people in one of three ways—individually, in small groups, or in large groups (such as the morning service or the congregational meeting). Each of these meetings offers a person an opportunity to be reconciled to his neighbor, to extend to him his warmth, his concern, his help, his understanding—in short, to be to him a brother in Christ.

The *large group meeting* has an important place in the life of a congregation. It is a time for celebration, corporate worship, decision making, and sharing information. For some matters, no other type of meeting will do. Festivals and family nights that are celebrations; congregational meetings that inform, report, transact business, or call a new minister; and worship that binds the community together in common commitment—all these are necessary meetings of the Christian church.

For other matters, large group meetings are not sufficient. There is little opportunity for face-to-face meeting between persons. There is little time for individual questions. Persons can remain observers, and often do. Observers are rarely transformed. Large group meetings should never be the only meetings that church members experience.

One of the great American preachers, Harry Emerson Fosdick, once compared preaching to a man standing on top of a ten-story building with an eyedropper trying to hit someone's diseased eye in the sea of upturned faces of the crowd below. Fosdick knew the limits of preaching. Words spoken by a preacher, even the best chosen words, will not always heal a hurt or restore a broken relationship.

Protestants in the sixteenth, seventeenth, and eighteenth centuries welcomed large meetings more than people do today. In those days, few people could read, very few other meetings were held, no television or radio was available, papers were rare, and news was transmitted primarily by word of mouth. In such a time most people literally hung on the preacher's every word, although the Pilgrims found it helpful to have a deacon on hand to prod those who showed signs of falling asleep. This was the only formal gathering for most of the congregation. Preaching provided not only the Good News but also the local news. Fellowship, education, and the answers to the questions people were asking were found in this large meeting and often in no other place. Today the large meeting of the church is simply one among many.

Three hundred years ago in England a minister by the name of Richard Baxter made a disturbing discovery. For twenty years he had preached, twice on Sundays and once during the week; but he was not satisfied with the religious life of the congregation. So one day he began calling in the homes. He was appalled by how little his members had actually learned about the Christian faith after all those years of preaching. Thereafter he undertook regular visitation and teaching in the homes, usually gathering the whole family around the kitchen table. He was gratified to discover that often far more was accomplished in that hour around the table with a family than in all of the years of his preaching. *The Reformed Pastor*[1] is a book Baxter wrote recounting these experiences that he felt demonstrated the need for more than one type of meeting in the church.

The *two-person meeting* is a second type always available in the church. Every person recalls critical times in his life when personal conversation with a spouse, a friend, a teacher, a parent, a minister, a fellow worker, or even with a stranger was very helpful. Personal conversation has always been an important kind of "meeting" for Christian witness. Jesus' encounters with persons comprised a significant aspect of his ministry. In like manner the individual care of souls has been central to the ministry of the church in all ages.

Thoughtful dialogue with another appeals to a person

---

[1] Turn to page 110 for the notes.

when he is in difficulty and needs help in understanding himself and his life. In personal conversation there is the privacy he needs. There is steadiness of encounter. There is eye contact. There is mutual responsibility. There is listening. More and more ministers are being trained in the skills and the spirit of personal conversation. Laymen need the training too. How can Christian love best be expressed as we listen, question, inform, and share with another person? How can one person be of most help to another person who seeks him out for conversation?

Churches need far more of this two-person type of meeting among all of the members. To be understood and accepted by another person, to be free to disclose ourselves fully to another person, is too rare an experience for many people these days. The rapid growth of the psychotherapeutic profession from whom many people "buy" listening indicates the great need. The restoration and revitalization of a one-to-one ministry could do much for the renewal of the church. Perhaps each church member should have a sponsor who makes himself available whenever he is needed. Such sponsorship would make concrete our responsibility for our brother. The "binding together" which is the very meaning of religion could then become personal experience. Christian meeting is superficial without authentic dialogue with significant other persons.

A third type of personal encounter is the *small group meeting*. We begin life in such a group: our family. All through life we are influenced by and even determined by the particular groups to which we belong. If we know the groups to which a person belongs, we are often helped in understanding what kind of a person he is. The gang, the youth group, the fraternity or sorority, and the club influence the person. We might say that we are our "belongings." We are accurately revealed by the groups to which we belong.

We have been *formed* by the groups to which we belonged in the past; we can be *transformed* by the groups to which we belong in the future. An example of this transforming power of the small group is the change in an adolescent when he leaves the family group and joins his fellow teenagers. The history of the church is filled with examples of the transforming power of small groups—Jesus and his disciples, Wesley and his meetings, the Pilgrims, and many of the small group beginnings of present-day denominations. If we could provide an equally significant belonging for our church members today, we could transform the church.

The work camp is a small group experience that often greatly transforms its members. Why? Work camps have a common enterprise. Members feel liable and responsible for one another. Communication is good. Trust and love are present even though members often engage in creative conflict with their ideas. Members feel increasingly free to disclose their real selves as they think and feel and work honestly together in the service of human need. In a short time the small group experience in a work camp develops a belonging that is significant for the members.

The main concern of this book is to help readers understand better the small groups to which they belong. As everyone knows, not every small group meeting is a huge success, not even when everyone talks. The church has often neglected to work at the task of making its small groups significant. It is hard work and we have not known how or where or when to begin. But begin we must if we are to grow together as fellow citizens with the saints in the household of God.

How a Small Group Functions

The small group is defined here as that number of persons who can enter into face-to-face relationship and can speak to one another in the course of a given meeting. Such a group numbers from three to fifteen persons. No more than that.

In every group meeting there are four aspects or systems that need to function adequately if the group is to be productive and rewarding for its members.

1. *Content* means "What is this meeting all about?" It is a mixture of business, discussion, ideas, and feelings. What the agenda is and what the secretary records in the minutes is what we usually think of as the content of a meeting. The one part of content often omitted in these records is the feelings that were present at the meeting. We are not very good at expressing feelings without feeling threatened. Although they are an important part of what goes on in any meeting—it may be the *most* important part—the feelings present at a meeting are often unrecognized and unresolved.

2. *Process* means "How is the group going about its task?" Process is the way the group handles the content and the way the members relate to one another. Asking a question, clarifying a previous statement, initiating discussion, and listening as well as speaking are all parts of the process of group life. Some of these activities we clearly recognize as process. Others we do not. Underneath the process, a relationship of trust is or is not present. And thereby hangs the group's life.

3. *Responsibility* means "Who is 'caring for' the life of this group?" Who is responsible for the content and the process systems in the group? Everyone? The leader? No one? Sometimes we know quite clearly; at other times no one seems to know or to care.

4. *Evaluation* means "How well is the group doing?" It is the appraisal of the group that everyone makes, consciously or unconsciously, during and after the meeting. Members make comments about the meeting to one another, to husbands and wives, or to themselves as they get ready for bed. Every group meeting is evaluated. Unfortunately for most groups, the evaluation does not take place within the meeting. Too often it takes place in the car going home

or over a cup of coffee next day, when it can do no one any good.

The malfunctioning of any or all of these aspects—content, process, responsibility, evaluation—accounts for the problems in many of our groups. Understanding and paying attention to these four systems will help us accomplish the purpose of our meetings, be it educational, administrative, or therapeutic.

These four aspects of group life are not new. The members of all small groups—committee, seminar, Bible study group, youth fellowship, women's circle, class, board, family—who live or work or study or meet together do so in terms of *content, process, responsibility,* and *evaluation.* They may not do it well—most do not—hence this book.

II

UNDERSTANDING
THE CONTENT

Meetings in the church are concerned with many kinds of content. We have to repair and renovate buildings, raise money and draw up budgets, find teachers and workers, design a building, plan programs, seek new members—in short, keep the institution going.

In searching for the best definition of the purpose of the church, Richard Niebuhr concluded that the simple language of Jesus—"You shall love the Lord your God with all your heart, and with all your soul, and with all your strength, and with all your mind; and your neighbor as yourself"—furnishes the best key to Jesus' own purpose and reveals the convictions of Jesus' life and of the early Christian community. *The real business of the church is "the increase among men of the love of God and neighbor."*[2]

Meetings that matter will include all kinds of agenda items related to keeping an institution going. They should also include relationships that reconcile man to God, and man to man. Unlike much of our experience, meetings in the church should serve to increase the love of God and the love of neighbor. The ministry of reconciliation is our basic business as Christians.

Whatever the obvious concern of a meeting, be it ushering, salaries, curriculum materials, open occupancy, or benevolences, other concerns are always present as part of the content of the meeting. They may not appear on the agenda but they affect the meeting greatly, sometimes even disastrously.

The content of a meeting includes all the words that are spoken and all the feelings that are felt. We are aware of the words that are spoken; in fact, we record them in the minutes. We pay little attention to the feelings that are present. We hide them, ignore them, or try to smooth them over. Rarely do we call them by name or treat them with respect. Disregarding feelings imperils our decisions and weakens our fellowship. Angry, hostile, hurt feelings do not go away. They often return in different guise to thwart the carrying out of the decisions of the majority and to estrange one man from another.

Few churches have completely escaped such rifts in the fellowship. They occur in decisions about the use of the church parlor as well as in decisions about a merger with another group of fellow Christians. It would seem that a rational, intelligent, objective decision could be made about each of these matters. That in many churches such decisions have not been made without bitterness and hard feelings underscores the principle of this chapter: *A meeting needs to be concerned with both ideas and feelings.*

Another way to think about this is to say: A meeting needs to be both impersonal and personal, both objective and subjective. That thought may be a little dismaying. Most of us do not expect church meetings to be personal matters; we expect impersonal objectivity and decisions of the majority to prevail. For working out details of room assignments, ushering, and budget, such objectivity is desirable; for increasing the love of man for God and for his neighbor, it is useless.

Take a Bible study group for example. Bible study groups usually begin with an impersonal discussion of ideas and a search for the correct interpretation of a passage. Members want to know what the commentaries, the experts, the authorities think. Until the Bible study group gets beyond the impersonal into personal content, the members will not experience the Bible as the living revelation of God. So long as the stories and teachings of the Bible remain simply historical fact having a correct interpretation, the Bible is a dead, inert book, as useless in daily living as a cookbook is to one who never intends to use it for cooking. Adequate response to the biblical story demands *my personal response.* The meeting will have to "get personal."

Biblical study of the two great commandments, "You shall love the Lord your God with all your heart, and with all your soul, and with all your strength, and with all your mind; and your neighbor as yourself" (Luke 10:27), may properly spend time with objective, impersonal discussion of these ideas. What was the history of these ideas in Jewish thought? What was their relevance in Jesus' day? But the content of the Bible study meeting is impoverished and falls short of its transforming possibilities if at some point the members do not say, "Now this is *my* witness about God and my neighbor. I am struggling in such-and-such ways to strengthen my love for my neighbor. In day-to-day life this is how it is with *my* soul, *my* heart, and *my* mind." Impersonal content alone in our meetings cannot contribute to "an

17

increase of the love of God and the love of neighbor." Such increase comes through personal response.

A meeting needs both "knowledge about" and "experience of" the Christian faith. Anyone who ever took swimming lessons can appreciate this distinction. The lessons could consist of knowledge about all of the swimming techniques, their history and development, and examples of their use. Theories about various strokes and their relative speeds could be discussed. The chemistry of water and its buoyancy could be analyzed. But swimming is never taught that way. If swimming lessons contained only "knowledge about" swimming the learner would complain bitterly, "What a terrible course. I haven't learned to swim! Let me get into the water and have the *experience* of swimming." We know that without this tryout in the water no one can learn to swim. Content in a swimming class clearly must be both "knowledge about" and "experience of" swimming.

Too many Christians know all about Christianity but they have no experience of being Christian, of acting as a Christian in matters of race relations, civil rights, world peace, poverty, death, family estrangements—or even in meetings at church. Church meetings often offer only "knowledge about" and no "experience of." Becoming a Christian means experiencing God's love and forgiveness, experiencing our neighbor's love and forgiveness, and experiencing the extending of our own love and forgiveness to a neighbor. It is not enough to know that love and forgiveness exist.

Evidence of the need for both knowledge about and experience of the Christian faith sometimes comes to a person who has studied the Bible and belonged to the church for years. One day a radical shift in his life—death, failure, betrayal, dishonesty—suddenly makes him realize for the first time how much he needs an experience of God's love and his neighbor's love. If, happily, someone extends such love and concern to him, without limit and with no expectation of reward, the parable of the prodigal son becomes a living truth. The person experiences in his own life the reconciliation portrayed in the parable. He no longer merely knows about the reconciliation, he has had the experience of being reconciled to God and to his neighbor.

A meeting must seek to serve the church both as an institution and as the Body of Christ. We have been accustomed to thinking of church meetings as necessities for the operation and maintenance of the church as an institution. So they are. We cannot be good stewards of our resources without planning for their proper care and use. But such concerns are *instrumental* only.

We must not lose sight of the original purpose of the church: the increase among men of the love of God and neighbor. Church meetings large and small, must provide for all who participate in the church's life opportunities for reconciliation, forgiveness, and belonging. This is our *fundamental* concern. Every meeting in the church needs to be concerned with both the instrumental and the fundamental content of the meeting.

The next time someone asks at the beginning of a meeting, "What shall we talk about tonight?" remember:

1. The *content* of a meeting is both ideas and feelings.
2. The *content* of a meeting should provide both knowledge about and experience of the Christian faith.
3. The *content* of a meeting should be both instrumental (plans and program for the church) and fundamental (the increase of love among men).

If you cannot remember all this, take this book to the meeting; then there will be something to talk about.

III

IMPROVING
THE PROCESS

One of the frequent sins of group life in the church is a failure of persons to understand and to care for one another. We strongly endorse Christian love, but we falter in our practice of it. We advocate forgiveness—even unto death—but we find it difficult to ask for and to grant. *How* we talk about the matters before us and *how* we behave toward each other as we move through the business of a meeting can and should be an experience of the faith that stresses love, acceptance, and forgiveness.

The process of a meeting is the way the group handles the content and the way the members relate to one another. Process refers to the interaction between members—the harmony, the friction, the jockeying, the cooperation.

Understanding the process of a meeting will enable us to be more helpful members of groups. When we know not only what is going on in a group but also how and why, we will be in a position to help the members of a group complete their business and minister to one another. It may be that the battle for the kingdom of God will be won or lost not in far-flung, worldwide action but in the meeting-by-meeting opportunities we all have to extend the ministry of reconciliation to one another in small groups. We are not supposed to wait for the Second Coming. We are called to minister to one another here, now, day by day, meeting by meeting.

Christians too often forget the history of the early church. Neither the Bible, nor the church as an institution, nor theology came into existence immediately after the death and resurrection of Jesus Christ. The *first* response of the disciples was to maintain and enlarge the fellowship (*koinonia* is the Greek word) that began with Jesus. The fellowship was an experience of living together in love. The members cared for one another. The members bore one another's burdens. They shared their possessions. They communicated openly and honestly with one another. They trusted one another. Those who belonged to the fellowship were no longer strangers and sojourners. They were at one with one another and with God. They were reconciled to one another and to God. Their love of one another and of God had been increased.

As the first generation of Jesus' followers began to die and as the disciples tried to tell those at a distance about their experiences, several things happened. In order to preserve the initial experiences they made records, they collected letters, and eventually their descendants canonized the Bible. In order to maintain the style and quality of the first Christian community, later Christians agreed upon certain rules and procedures, and the church as an institution began to take shape. Different interpretations of the experiences, the Bible, and the church were present among the members. These interpretations (theology) became part of the ethos of the church.

Note that the Bible, the church, and theology are secondary and always point beyond themselves to the more important experiences of love of God and fellowmen. As present-day churchmen, we cannot rest content with knowing the Bible, maintaining the institutional church, and proclaiming a correct theology. These activities may help us come to the experience of reconciliation, but they are no substitute for it. Paying attention to the dynamics of the process in our meetings gives us a concrete way of improving our relationships with one another and being reconciled to one another. Such an increase in our love of neighbor increases our love of God. For God's love is made known to us through persons who are followers of Jesus Christ. "If anyone says, 'I love God,' and hates his brother, he is a liar; for he who does not love his brother whom he has seen, cannot love God whom he has not seen" (1 John 4:20).

STRATEGIES OF GROUP PROCESS

A *positive strategy* is a specific act that helps the group. Out of the thirty or forty strategic actions that might be present in a meeting, six basic ones are given below.

1. *Initiating* is the strategy of starting things. This is a much needed process which is customarily maintained by a chairman, although it can be performed by any of the members. Calling the meeting to order, proposing an agenda item, raising a question, changing the direction of the discussion, and introducing a new idea are all examples of the strategy of initiating.

2. *Integrating* the ongoing discussion in order to make apparent a common thread in the discussion is highly useful. Without this process of integration or "linking together," a small group meeting can be a very individualistic affair. At

any point in a meeting there may be three or four ideas, suggestions, or questions before the group at the same time. Someone needs to call attention to this fact so that the members of the group can work together.

3. *Sharing information* is necessary if the group is to make intelligent decisions in the light of all the known facts. If members withhold necessary information for any reason—the information is too personal, too emotional, too controversial; or the members are too threatened, too lazy, or too selfish—the meeting is impoverished.

4. *Clarifying* is the restatement of contributions in such a way as to sharpen their meaning and make them more understandable to the group.

5. *Testing* is the strategy by which a member checks to ascertain the group's readiness for a vote, its willingness to change the subject, its feelings about the time available, or its interest or its present position in the subject matter under discussion. Often group meetings wander aimlessly around and around a subject because no member provides the process of testing.

6. *Summarizing* the discussion puts before the group a possible conclusion, thus allowing the members to agree or disagree and to move ahead in their meeting.

This partial list suggests the nature of the positive strategies that are a necessary part of any meeting. Some other strategies are *negative,* often expressing self-centeredness and self-seeking motives. In order to be understood, accepted, and worked through by the group, negative strategies must be recognized. For that reason the following examples have been included here.

1. *Blocking* stops or stalls the actions of a group. Irrelevant argument without listening, rejection of ideas without consideration, ignoring some contributions, stubborn asser-

tion of a position, threatening the group—all of these tactics can effectively block a meeting.

2. *Domination* of the discussion by one person or by a few persons can permanently damage the life of a group. The other members will rebel and become aggressive. Or they will conform and become submissive. Aggression and submission in response to domination will not produce a meeting that matters to its members. The temptation to dominate is strong in persons of status, in persons who are insecure and uncertain about their position in the group, and in persons who feel inferior. They cover up by acting superior to others or by dominating other members.

3. *Withdrawing* is a negative strategy often revealed by silence. Sometimes silence is golden, but prolonged silence on the part of a member can be a threat to the group. Not knowing what the silent person is thinking, the other members become uneasy. Another way a person can withdraw from the immediate task of the group is by diverting the attention of some members with a side conversation or with an ill-timed joke.

Let us now look at a meeting in which the basic positive strategies are operating.

The chairman of a board of deacons *initiates* an item of business. "It's time to plan our special lenten program again. What suggestions do you have?"

Mr. Tuck responds: "I was bored by last year's speaker. I don't see why we put time and money into a lenten program."

Mrs. Jones *clarifies* Mr. Tuck's statement: "You don't want to work on another lenten program unless it's better than last year."

"That's right. I'm not against Lent, but I am against boring programs," says Mr. Tuck.

Mr. Peters *shares information*: "A church I know always appoints a group of laymen to talk with the speaker ahead of time about the interests and questions of the congregation. The speaker is briefed about what will be boring and what will be of interest."

At this point Mr. Williams says: "What is the purpose of Lent, anyway?" Such a question could *block* action by the group. If this member is *dominating,* he can hold up serious discussion of the coming lenten program by joking or debunking or telling about his childhood experiences with Lent or by using other diversionary tactics.

But Mr. Peters *integrates* this question into the general discussion. "Many of our church members have the same question. We come from many denominations. Why can't our lenten program deal with the purpose of Lent? We could meet with the speaker ahead of time and make certain he understands our questions." *(This is summarizing and testing.)*

Chairman: "Are you ready to make that a motion for formal action?"

Mr. Roberts volunteers: "I will, after we hear from Mr. James. He hasn't spoken all evening and I want to know what he thinks before I vote." Mr. James' silent *withdrawal* threatens Mr. Roberts who speaks for himself and for the group.

Mr. James says: "I'm sorry if my silence has bothered you this evening. Actually I've been with you all the way. I move the recommendation proposed by Mr. Peters."

The meeting isn't over at this point, but the strategies necessary for a productive meeting are operating.

COMMUNICATION AND GROUP PROCESS

Three steps are necessary to complete an act of communication: expression, listening, and response. Unless all three steps are completed we cannot be certain that communication has taken place.

Tape recordings made by seminary students of meetings

in which they participated provide many illustrations of a breakdown in communication. Expressions lack clarity and conciseness. Listening is careless and partial. Response is often nonexistent. In fact, some meetings consist almost entirely of one new expression after another, each one ignoring the ideas and feelings that have already been expressed. Paying attention to how well we are communicating in any small group meeting can make the difference between a good meeting and a poor one. Good communication helps to make conflict creative rather than destructive. Making sure that communication is occurring in the midst of an argument calms tempers. Many times persons discover that the conflict diminishes or even disappears when they take the time to listen, to understand, and to respond to the other person. Communication is a two-way process. One-way expression is only the beginning of the act of communication.

STEP ONE: *Expression* seems simple, something we are all able and only too willing to do. Yet the ability to reveal our thoughts and feelings with clarity is difficult. We cannot take it for granted. Furthermore, before we express our thoughts, we have to make some decisions. Are we going to express our thoughts *and* our feelings? Are we going to express our opinions or the opinions held by other people? Are we going to express something of our own interior life or keep the discussion more objective? All of these kinds of expression are useful in their proper places. Each time we speak we decide how much of ourselves to disclose. Meetings that matter are not "games of verbal ping-pong" in which interesting opinions on odd topics are batted back and forth. Meetings that matter require authentic expressions from each member.

Different kinds of expression are illustrated by the following transcript of part of a Bible study group meeting in an inner-city church.

1. Mrs. Jones: I believe prayer can change people, rather than more or less changing things. Most people just think prayer changes things. Like sometimes when people's attitude is changed. I think prayer changes people as well as things. It can change people and things.

2. Pastor: The function of prayer, then, is to change the inward and spiritual life of a person as well as things.

3. Mrs. Jones: Yes.

4. Mrs. Ralph: Well, I think even though we don't see prayer changing things now, it may be that in prayer we strengthen our faith.

5. Pastor: Prayer for you is a central part of the Christian experience.

6. Mrs. Ralph: Uh huh.

7. Mrs. Jones: I think that if you believe in Jesus Christ, then you won't pray for things to happen as we ourselves might want them. That's selfish anyway. But in prayer sometimes you think it's somebody else, but it might all lie in you. After thoughtful prayer you get a different light on it. Sometimes little things in you change and then people may change toward you.

8. Pastor: Are you saying something like "our lives may be the only Bible some people will read?"

9. Mrs. Jones: I've heard that before.

10. Pastor: Is that what you are trying to say?

11. Mrs. Jones: Not in a sense, but it has something to do with that. But, yes, for when you go to church people expect you to act differently. You'll never get anyone to be a Christian if you don't set an example. You've got to more or less live differently besides just going to church and saying you believe.

12. Pastor: A big part of the Christian faith is that it makes a difference in your life.

13. Mrs. Jones: Yeah, I think so, don't you?

14. Pastor: Yes, I think it's got to make a difference or it really isn't a faith.

Mrs. Jones, at 1 and 7, is honestly expressing part of her unsophisticated Christian faith and witness. Mrs. Ralph at 4 makes one expression of her belief. The pastor does not express his own beliefs in this exchange. He tries to understand what these women are saying. But Mrs. Jones' comment at 11 indicates that he has not succeeded. She keeps trying to express what she means.

STEP TWO: *Listening.* The pastor is trying very hard to listen to these women and to understand what they are saying. The difficulty of adequately completing an act of communication becomes apparent here. The pastor's remark at 8 changes the subject, although he probably did not intend to do that. Prayer is not mentioned again. In the midst of trying hard to listen, the pastor was apparently racing his mind in an attempt to say something important. This is a temptation every listener faces. It is hard work to concentrate on the expressions of another person. The pastor's quotation was somewhat useful but it did not indicate that he had heard all that was on Mrs. Jones' mind as she struggled with the ways of prayer.

From the cartoons in our daily papers to the midnight psychiatric advice on television, we are made aware these days of the importance of listening. The need to talk with someone who will listen is great, but listeners are in short supply. More and more people seek out professionals who will listen for a price. Thus the plain fact is that the discipline of listening is not easy and we are often too self-concerned to give ourselves completely to understanding what the other person is saying. When members of a group—say the members of a board of trustees—are trying to communicate with one another, there is the added temptation to think that someone else will listen. Often no one does.

Listening goes on at a variety of levels in our meetings. *A first level of listening is with our ears only.* We are polite and our facial expression and our bodily stance indicate to the other person that we are listening, but "it ain't necessarily so." Our reply, after listening with our ears only, may indicate that we have not adequately heard the other person. Our ears were within earshot; but our interior ear—that is, our mind—was thinking about something else. Perhaps we tuned out the speaker entirely. This is the frustration often depicted by the cartoon in which the husband is giving the proper answers while his wife speaks to him, but when she looks up from her kitchen counter he is actually reading the newspaper. Such polite listening makes us angry, anytime, anywhere, at home or in a committee meeting.

A second level can be characterized as listening with the mind. When we listen with our mind we hear what has been said, think about it in relation to our own ideas and convictions, and respond in such a way that the speaker will know that he has been heard. Listening with the mind is the backbone of good committee meetings and vigorous study groups. Education, science, industry, politics, religion—the life of the world—are dependent upon man's ability to listen with his mind.

A pitfall in this level of listening occurs when a person's mind always works as in a debate to win his point without adequately taking into account the other person's viewpoint. His mind hears only enough to allow him to formulate his side of the argument. We frustrate the creative function of listening if we continually operate in a mood of trying to impress or disrupt or get the better of the other person. Listening with the mind is at its best when persons are intent upon understanding one another's ideas about a common concern.

Listening with the heart is the third level. Here we are listening not only for the objective discussion but also for the very sake and being of the other person. By listening with the heart we mean paying strictest attention to another. We listen without judgment or criticism or superiority, but with love. We try hard to understand the world from the point of view of the speaker. We put ourselves in the shoes of the other person. Such listening with an open heart and mind *feels* the grief, the loneliness, the despair, the hurt, the doubts of that person. When there is this kind of listening, a person may reveal secrets that have been a source of anxiety and a lonely burden for years. He knows that he is at one with his hearer, that there is no need to keep up pretenses. He can speak honestly, knowing that he will be understood and accepted.

Listening with the heart is evidence of the deep commitment of one person to another. It is treating him with profound respect and granting him significance and worth. It is, in fact, loving him. It may be that such listening cannot be sold, but only given away. The earliest church had this "listening with the heart" available in its fellowship. It was this which caused men and women to marvel at the communion and the community that was present in their midst. In our churches today we can also become "members one of another" if we care enough to listen.

STEP THREE: *Response* completes the communication process by demonstrating, through restatement in the listener's own words, that the expression of the first speaker has been understood. We often assume that we have adequately heard another person's expression and that there is no need for a verbal response. This is a mistake.

Without response, which the original speaker can correct if our listening has been faulty, the group may proceed in a meeting with an incorrect understanding. Without response, which gives evidence that the listener has truly understood, the speaker may remain in doubt. Evidence both from diaries kept by group members and from analyses of many meetings indicates that the person who repeats himself every ten minutes often is a person who has not been understood. Tension builds up in him; he makes his point again and again. The other members of the group are increasingly bored because they have heard his speech before. But until someone acknowledges it satisfactorily, they are likely to hear the speech yet another time.

Response is related to the strategy of clarification in that it helps the group to understand better the contribution that is being made. A thoughtful or questioning response often helps the original speaker state more clearly what he is trying to say.

Groups can demonstrate the inadequacy of most communication for themselves by following this formula for a time: *"Each person can speak up for himself only after he has first restated the ideas and feelings of the previous speaker accurately, and to that speaker's satisfaction."*[3] Only after an acceptable response can the second person go on to make his point. This forced listening and response slows down the meeting and puts high priority on understanding. Invariably a number of members cannot restate the previous speaker's expression. This shows that even when we try, we are often unable to listen very well. If there is conflict or rigorous debate in the group, this mechanical rule evens the tempers and increases the chances of mutual understanding. It does not guarantee conformity. It does guarantee respect and a hearing for each person. It is difficult to maintain hostility when each person has had demonstrated the fact that someone has listened and responded to him. Try it in your next meeting!

Disturbances of communication are at the root of many of our most troublesome problems—mental illness, marital estrangement, community squabbles, international fear and distrust. Many of men's problems can be laid at the door of faulty communication. The problems of small group meetings are no exception. Often they occur because completed acts of communication are lacking. Expression, listening, and response—which together make up the process of communication—are the lifeblood of a meeting. If this kind of completed communication process is not present in our meetings, the meetings are a violation of our Christian intention and commitment. Man was created to live in relationship to God and neighbor. Such relationship can only be sustained by adequate communication.

Trust: The Basis of Open, Honest Group Life

The fellowship and reconciliation we seek in the church depends upon a basic climate of trust. In fact, trust is basic to all human relationships. The baby develops a sense of basic trust or, tragically, mistrust from the experiences of his first year of life.[4] The child who learns from his initial experiences that he cannot trust the persons around him is likely to grow up suspicious of his boss, his wife, his parents, and his friends. Believing that the world is against him, he may become aggressive and hostile, always looking out for himself, with little awareness of or concern for the rights and feelings of others. Or he may be like a walled city; all you get to know of such a person is the height and thickness of his wall. He looks out, but he reveals little of how things are going inside. His mistrust prevents him from getting close to anyone or sharing his real concerns with anyone; he is lonely and isolated.

By contrast, the child who discovers that the persons around him are trustworthy grows into an adult who is warm, open, and spontaneous. He is able to relate to people; he has close friends; he uses his energy for work and for love instead of protecting and hiding himself.

The marriage relationship further illustrates the importance of trust. No marriage can long endure if the partners do not trust each other. When trust is lacking, both husband and wife become guarded in what they say and what they do. Communication breaks down and no positive strategy will repair it. When there is lack of trust, there is lack of caring. Husband and wife are suspicious, defensive, and estranged. Soon the marriage exists in name only.

Trust is also basic to the relationships that exist in a small group meeting. When trust is absent, strategies—even positive strategies intended to be helpful—are seen as manipulation. When trust is absent, members become suspicious, hostile, isolated, and on guard. No one commits himself, his ideas, or his feelings in an atmosphere of mistrust.

By contrast, when a climate of trust pervades a meeting, members can set about doing the work of the meeting with vigor, honesty, and real pleasure. Members can then work out disagreements without rupturing the basic relationship, without fear of losing face, and without suspicion of the motives of others.

There is a phenomenon of small group meetings which a climate of trust allows a group to recognize and deal with. "Hidden agenda" is the term that describes this occurrence. Any person who has something on his mind—a concern, a conviction, or a personal problem—which influences what he says or does in a meeting is said to have a hidden agenda. It is hidden because what concerns him is not known to the group. Consequently, the other members do not understand why he is so insistent or "pushy" or repetitive or withdrawn.

In a weekly Bible study group, Mrs. Williams kept questioning love and forgiveness. "The Bible is too idealistic. Times are different than they were in Jesus' day. Forgiveness is a good idea, but it won't work. People take advantage of you." The group listened again and again.

During the sixth session she revealed her hidden agenda. Mrs. Williams and her husband were having trouble. She had been holding her husband's past misbehavior against him. She had been unwilling to forgive him because this would mean giving up her means of trying to control him. Trust was at a low ebb in their marriage.

Until the day she trusted the Bible study group enough to share this hidden agenda, her opinions and questions about forgiveness seemed cynical and needlessly time-consuming to the other members. When her hidden agenda was made known to the group, the members were able to be more helpful and understanding.

Many persons bring a hidden agenda to meetings, waiting —even hoping—for the time to come when they can share their personal concerns with the group. A seventeen-year-old boy sits through endless youth meetings wondering if he can trust the group enough to share his concern about death and the suicide of his grandfather. A trustee serves the church for years as chairman of the building committee while he keeps hidden his concerns about the ethical practices in his corporation. A fourth grader in the church school hides the fact that he never gets any breakfast on Sunday morning. He just gets shoved out of the house. A deacon does not agree with certain biblical interpretations by the minister but never trusts the board of deacons enough to raise his questions at a meeting. A minister seeks to help the people of his church achieve an abundant, creative, full life, but he does not reveal his anxieties about his own life as he faces retirement.

A member with a hidden agenda hopes that the group will help him. But he must share the hidden agenda before the group can help, and this he often hesitates to do. Often he works on the hidden agenda, as Mrs. Williams did, without telling the group about it. Participating in a group agenda primarily in terms of the private pressures or personal problems of a hidden agenda can be disrupting and puzzling to the other group members.

How can you, as a member of a church board, committee, or study group, act so that trust becomes the fabric of your group life? Sermonizing about the virtue of trust between man and man, and between man and God, will not prove very helpful when it comes to trusting the people in a particular group.

An attitude of *acceptance* is the cornerstone for the building of trust. To accept a person is to grant him significance and worth; it is to treat him with respect and courtesy. Acceptance is *not* saying: "You're right, I agree with you" (when you actually do not). Acceptance is saying (for example): "You feel that forgiveness is an overrated virtue. I do not agree with you, but I want to understand why you feel that way."

To accept a person is to be able to hear and feel and

understand strong feelings—hostility, bitterness, cynicism, and grief as well as the happier expressions of joy, delight, love, and warmth—without scorning, ignoring, rejecting, or condemning him for having these feelings.

We do not always do well when we try to accept persons. Strong expressions of unpleasant feelings shock us or attack us, and we often respond in kind. Then the fat's in the fire and trust goes up in smoke.

Trust grows in any human relationship where persons show themselves to be trustworthy. Perhaps that is where we need to begin in our meetings and in our fellowship. When we can accept each person just as he is, without offending him or being offended by him, we shall show ourselves to be worthy of his trust. Then communication becomes open and honest, strategies for working together become skilled tools of group life, and the process of our life together bears witness to the love of God.

IV

ACCEPTING
THE RESPONSIBILITY

If you are a member of a small group meeting that does not seem to matter to anyone, who is to blame? If you are a member of a committee meeting that rambles along aimlessly, who is to blame? If you are a member of a study group that is frustrating, boring, irrelevant, and unproductive, who is to blame? Most of the time we blame the leader, or a dominating person, or the materials, or someone else. But the only answer that makes sense for free men and women is: "Each member bears a responsibility." A leader may have more initial responsibility; but every member begins to share that responsibility when he chooses to come to the meeting.

A Bible study group of young adults discovered their individual responsibility for their meeting as the result of a chance question by their leader. At the beginning of the fourth session one of the members asked the leader a question about the interpretation of a biblical passage. The leader paused before making his usual quick reply.

"Do we have agreement in the group that this is the question we all want answered now?"

Expecting nods of agreement, the leader was surprised when someone said: "No, we are not agreed."

The leader was even more surprised by what happened during the next hour and a half. Everybody jumped into the discussion with ideas about how the group should be conducted. Feelings of resentment toward the leader were expressed. Two members, including the one who asked the original question, were criticized for dominating the discussion. They both apologized; but in defense, they said that no one else seemed to have anything to say. This brought a denial from several members who had been silent until then. They said that there had been almost no space in the discussion when anyone who was the slightest bit slow could have spoken. Two people said they had been bored and they had wondered how they could get out of the group gracefully. Some of the young adults had been together in a previous group. They confessed that they had continued their relationship in this group as if they were still in the old group, with little regard for the newcomers.

The Bible study group did not discuss the Bible any more that night. They did discuss each member's responsibility to the group. As a result of the unexpected discussion that evening, responsibility passed from the leader to all the members. It was no longer the leader's group. The group belonged to everyone. The members were responsible for the group, for themselves, and for one another.

The Mature Person Is a Responsible Person

An increasing ability to be responsible for himself marks the development of a person from infancy to maturity. A baby is totally irresponsible. Those around him, primarily his mother, take full charge of his life. Through the years of childhood and adolescence we expect him to change from a dependent infant to an independent, responsible adult. Going to school alone, participating in the Scouts, staying away overnight for the first time, preparing an evening meal when mother is gone, and holding his first job are all signs of the child's increasing responsibleness. His happiness in marriage and his success in his vocation—in fact, all of the relationships during his whole life—are affected by his ability to be responsible.

Being free, persons can choose *not* to be fully responsible for themselves. However, being irresponsible brings trouble. Man is only really free when he is responsible. The minute a man chooses not to be responsible in some area of his life, someone takes away his freedom by exercising responsibility for him. Recovered alcoholics, members of Alcoholics Anonymous, know what happens when they become irresponsible. The wife of an alcoholic increasingly assumes many of the duties around the house, and with the children, which normally are her husband's. When the husband-and-father stops drinking, he is astonished at how much freedom he has lost. The long road to recovery includes not only being able to live without alcohol but also learning how to live responsibly in one's family and community.

Emotionally troubled persons who become hospitalized and delinquents who are institutionalized are immature persons. One of the clearest marks of their immaturity is their irresponsibility. They have chosen to act in ways that are unacceptable to their families and their society. They may blame others for the irresponsibility, but society nevertheless holds them responsible by detaining them. Troubled persons and delinquents are on the way to recovery when they begin to take responsibility for themselves and their behavior.

The story of a delinquent girl, Linda, reported by Dr. William Glasser,[5] illustrates the importance of acting responsibly. Linda was a sixteen-year-old girl who had been in and out of various institutions for three years. She had been charged with the use of narcotics, prostitution, attempted suicide, fighting, and general incorrigibility. These institutions had excused Linda's behavior because she was "emotionally disturbed." Linda learned to blame everyone else for her problems—parents, school, society, doctors. She was not responsible. It was not her fault. "After all we were emotionally disturbed and high strung delinquents and this made anything and all we did excusable." So Linda remained irresponsible and a problem to herself and to others. One day she struck a staff member and found herself transferred to a new institution, the Ventura School for Girls. In her own words she tells what was different here and how it changed her.

> These people had an extremely different attitude toward the girls. So you were emotionally disturbed, so big deal! There wasn't anything that anyone but you could do about it, so why worry. . . . I found a doctor who was less interested in what you had done and your past than he was in your immediate and far future. He was a very personable man and he gave you the feeling that he was interested in you, but not what you had done and never implied that there was any reason to ask why, as there was no fact necessary but that you did it and that was the reason for your present confinement. However, there was not any excuse for what you had done and you were to hold no one responsible for your acts but you. This is good, for it makes you accept responsibility for your actions rather than giving the fault to everyone who helped compose your environment.
>
> Now I am leaving this institution. . . . I have learned that I

cannot alter the past, but that I control my future and the responsibility lies solely with me as to my future.

Being responsible is the mark of a mature person.

THE CHRISTIAN IS A RESPONSIBLE PERSON

Christianity has always held persons accountable for their behavior. Jesus taught that a man was responsible for his life and for his relationship to his neighbor. When troubled persons came to Jesus for help, he did not suggest that they blame others for their predicament or that they wait for someone else to rescue them. Jesus encouraged persons in difficulties of all kinds to act responsibly. He taught them not to stay at the altar worshiping if they were in trouble with a brother, but to take the responsibility to go to that brother and straighten the trouble out—then come and praise God.

In Jesus' parable about the talents, the persons rewarded were those who used their talents responsibly. They were called "good and faithful." The person who was afraid and "buried" his talent lost even that which he had. Responsible behavior increases one's ability to be responsible. Uncertain, fearful, dependent, irresponsible behavior increases irresponsibility.

Martin Luther felt that the people of his day had become irresponsible in their religious life.[6] They were dependent upon the church. Luther put it bluntly: "Every man must do his own believing, just as every man must do his own dying." Responsibility is at the heart of the Christian faith as Protestants understand it.

The important Reformation idea—the priesthood of all believers—fixes our responsibility. The phrase does not mean that "every man is his own priest," giving us cause for individuality and isolation. It means the opposite, "Every man must be a priest to every other man." Luther said that a Christian is one who has faith in Christ and acts "reciprocally and mutually one the Christ of the other, doing to our neighbor as Christ does to us." Here is the Protestant root and obligation for each member's responsible participation in a meeting.

Each man must do his own believing but he does so in the context of his community, not in splendid isolation. God, neighbor, and self are inextricably bound together. Who can say precisely how God's reconciliation was mediated to him? The interdependence of all our lives suggests that God has spoken to us through many different persons in the course of our development from infancy. In our Christian witness "every man may be useful or beneficial to the rest." By this common priesthood, "we are able to appear before God, to pray for others, and to teach one another mutually the things that are of God . . . a Christian does not live for himself, but in Christ and his neighbor."

It follows, then, that all members of the church are responsible, not just the clergy. Protestants have acted on this conviction with varying degrees of success ever since the Reformation. Early Protestant church groups in Geneva, the Pietists, the Moravian Church under Count Zinzendorf, and the Methodists made themselves available to one another for mutual exhortation, counsel, and brotherly discipline. Present-day churchmen overlook, underestimate, and ignore one of the most obvious places for the exercise of our Christian responsibility: the small group meeting.

Shared Responsibility: Mark of a Christian Group

For church meetings of all kinds, the goal must be shared responsibility. No one can be mature for another member. No one can be Christian for another member. No one can participate in a group for another member. Groups are strong and resourceful, lively and interesting, and rewarding to all members *to the extent that each member is a responsible participant.*

During the first meetings of a small group there is often very little shared responsibility. Each member must decide whether or not he is going to involve himself responsibly in the group. The designated leadership must be particularly sensitive and concerned to foster growth in shared responsibility, lest the group remain at an immature, dependent level. The following excerpts from a diary by a seminary student tell of his experiences in being part of a group that was forced to take responsibility for its own life. He reflects on the kind of leadership necessary for this to happen.

Looking back I realize that I was helped to see my own irresponsibility and to see how much the success of the group depends on its members and not on the leader. In the early meetings I was terribly frustrated. I suspect all of us were frustrated and confused and we began to look for solutions, in fact we tried them out, picking solutions that would relieve us of responsibility. But quietly and surely our leader would not let us off the hook. And now I am grateful.

Too often in the past in my own leadership experiences, I have not entrusted responsibility to the group because I did not really think the group was capable of handling it and because I felt insecure in any position other than that of an authoritarian leader. I have seen in part the responsibility which a leader has for helping his members to realize their own creative potential for good and to help them solve their own problems as individuals and as groups.

There are three patterns of responsibility in meetings. As we consider the meetings in our churches, we find variations of these patterns depending upon the age of the members, how long the group has been meeting, its purpose, and the degree of group maturity.

1. *A leader (or clique) is responsible.* In some groups the leader (or a few persons) is responsible for the group's life. He knows what the plans are. He initiates the business. The members communicate primarily with the leader, not with one another. The leader is the authority.

Under this responsibility pattern, members feel dependent and helpless. Sometimes they rebel, becoming aggressive toward the leader and toward one another. With responsibility taken away from them, members try to retaliate as best they can by arguing, quitting, or blocking the task. Not sharing the information held by the leader, the members become suspicious and distrustful.

Sometimes members accept this pattern of responsibility because it allows them to remain irresponsible. Someone else is making the decisions. Not being responsible in the decision making, the members do not feel very responsible about anything else either. The leader can be blamed for everything that goes wrong.

If the leader is absent, the group does not know what to do. The members have not had the experience of being responsible and they are unprepared for taking responsibility.

This is an authoritarian situation. It is not to be confused with a situation in which the members of a group give limited responsibility to the leader or to another member for some aspect of the group's life—lecture, planning, or chairmanship. Such group decisions are an acceptable way of sharing responsibility.

There are many variations of authoritarian leadership. In one of the common ones, a beloved father figure or a benevolent dictator in many subtle and gracious ways takes the responsibility for the group's life from the members. The church is particularly vulnerable in this situation. People are always polite in the church. Everybody is nice. It is much harder to cope with a nice "authority" who is taking too much responsibility.

A clique—officers, vocal members, older members—may take responsibility and exercise power without proper authority. The more talkative, knowledgeable, dominating, and aggressive persons take charge at the expense of and without the consent of the quiet, uncertain, polite members. The effect on the group is the same as if authority were exercised by one person. The relationships are strained; the group morale is low; no love is lost.

2. *No one is responsible.* Sometimes no person in a group feels responsible, not even the leader. Each person does what he wants to do with little concern for anyone else. This is anarchy. If it persists very long, there will be no group. The members will separate.

With no responsibility being taken for the group, the members, pursuing their own designs, may begin bickering and disagreeing among themselves. Or they may become tired of waiting for someone to get them organized and stop coming to the meetings. Mutual trust, a sense of belonging, serious communication will not develop in such a group as this.

A variation on this pattern of responsibility occurs when a group with some cohesion of its own places major responsibility for what its members are doing on someone or something beyond the group's membership. "Headquarters" is a convenient place of anonymous persons who can be used as scapegoats. "They" at "headquarters" are responsible for what we are trying to do. There is a ready-made excuse for all irresponsible behavior in the local group: "They never understand the local situation." Rightly or wrongly, many a denominational program of evangelism, stewardship, teacher-training, or curriculum implementation has failed because the members of the local churches did not accept their responsibility for making it work and because the national staff members were unable to share the responsibility for the creation of the program.

Any group is in trouble that falls into a meeting pattern in which no one is responsible or in which its members blame someone outside the group for what it is doing. It will not make much difference in the lives of its members or in the life of the church. That group might just as well stop meeting and save on the light bill.

3. *Every person is responsible.* In a third kind of group, responsibility for the group's life and activity belongs to the

group itself. There are probably very few small group meetings (or churches) this side of heaven in which every member feels and acts responsibly. But most groups can do better than they have done in the past.

In the third group pattern, each member feels obligated to speak up, to facilitate communication, to contribute ideas, to encourage others, and to make suggestions for the group's procedure. Decisions, even if not unanimous, are talked through until every member accepts the verdict. As a consequence, all of the members feel that they have a personal commitment to the group task. All of the members rejoice when their plans succeed and are disappointed when they fail. They share the credit and they accept the blame.

This responsibility pattern builds strong relationships of trust and communication among the members. *Each member,* not just the leader, takes responsibility for himself and his neighbors. He cares for them, he respects them, he values them, he encourages them to act responsibly with him.

Shared responsibility is democracy in action. Shared responsibility is also Christian doctrine in action. It is a way of living and working together that affirms our love of neighbor and of God.

There is a lot to be done in a meeting—the maintenance of necessary strategies, the encouragement of communication, the fostering of trust, the marshaling of resources. The work will be most adequately done if all members share the load.

The responsibility pattern of a group needs to be examined, discussed, and understood by all; it should also be changed when the members feel that is necessary. One reason for ineffective group life in our churches today is that too many of us are not acting as responsible churchmen. We are embarrassed to discuss it. We do not face the question of who is responsible. Leaders are too insecure to ask for the discussion. Members know that if they raise the issue they may have to take responsibility. It is safer not to get involved. The net effect is small group meetings that are not very democratic, not very Christian, and not very helpful to any of us in our growth toward Christian maturity.

How persons in small groups can evaluate and improve what they are doing as well as how they are doing it is the subject of the next chapter.

V

PROFITING
FROM THE EVALUATION

Evaluation is the appraisal of a meeting by the members. Was it a good meeting, a poor meeting, or didn't it matter one way or another?

Too often evaluation takes place after the meeting is over. On the way home a member thinks to himself, "What a waste of time that meeting was! Why did ten people have to worry through every detail of the schedule, name tags, and table arrangements for the family night. A committee of three or four could have done it better." Disgusted, he wonders if all the boards of the church function like this one.

Or he may go out for coffee with one or two other members after the meeting and talk the whole thing over. If he meets another member downtown the next day, he is likely to find the conversation turning to the meeting again.

Meetings are always evaluated, one way or another.

You can tell how members evaluate a meeting by their actions. One person may stop attending because "I no longer have the time." Another dissatisfied member discovers several others who share his opinion. They meet together and plan a strategy which, they expect, will improve things. They become a clique within the group. Still other members reveal how they feel about the group by the way in which they work—or don't work—to help the group carry out its plan and programs. If they drag their feet or make excuses, they are clearly not in sympathy with the group's decisions. They think the group is wrong, or bumbling, or unimportant in what it is doing.

The trouble with all these varieties of private evaluation is that they are seldom helpful to the group. When judgments are made outside the meeting, the group cannot profit from them. It is only when critical or reflective comment by a group member is heard by the group that something can be done about it.

A seminary student reported an experience of a church school teachers' meeting in which an evaluation session, although unplanned, proved to be the beginning of better meetings. It was a meeting early in the fall. Twelve teachers assembled at eight o'clock that evening and the superintendent conducted the meeting. He talked about a number of things: announcements of coming events in the life of the church, how to keep attendance records, arrangement of the classrooms, use of the library, and on and on. The teachers said very little. One dozed. The meeting adjourned promptly at nine thirty and the group gathered in an adjoining room over a cup of coffee.

Three members who were talking together discovered that each one wished he had not come. One had a sick child at home; the second had a visiting mother-in-law; and the third said that she would have been further ahead if she had spent the time studying her church school lesson. All agreed that the meeting had been a waste of time.

To their chagrin, the superintendent overheard the trio. But instead of becoming defensive, he joined in the evaluation. He too was disappointed in the meeting and did not want to be responsible for another one of the same kind. As they talked, others joined the conversation. Consequently, the group had a second meeting which was an evaluation of the first one. At eleven o'clock they went home, their morale high about their teaching and their relationship to one another. They had experienced mutual trust and respect in their working together and were looking forward with real anticipation to their next meeting.

Evaluation does not have to be unplanned and it does not have to take place after the meeting is adjourned. In fact, to get the most out of it, evaluation should be a regular part of the meeting.

There are many ways you can learn to evaluate your meetings. One way is simply for a member—you—to step outside the group, figuratively speaking, and to make an observation about the group's process. "We are spending too much time on the details for family night. Let's depend on the subcommittee to complete the plans so that we can get on with our other business." This evaluative statement, followed by a positive strategy proposal, helps a group take stock of itself.

Another way is to use a checklist. When you plan to use such an instrument to help in the evaluation of your meeting, you must allow time for it, at least forty-five minutes the first time you introduce it. Once you become familiar with it, you may find that half an hour at the close of the business portion of your meeting will be as much time as you need. Eventually, as the members of your group become skilled in understanding one another's feelings and in

CHRISTIAN GROUP LIFE*

This is a checklist to help you evaluate your meeting and to increase sensitivity to some of the relationships in the life of the Christian community of faith.

Check the number on the rating scale that corresponds to your evaluation of the meeting in each of the following cate-gories. For example, if you feel that re-sponsible participation was lacking, check 1; if you feel that responsible participation was present, check 7; if you feel that the responsible participation of the group was somewhere in between, check an appro-priate number on the scale.

1   2   3   4   5   6   7

A. RESPONSIBLE PARTICIPATION
was lacking. We served our own needs. We watched from outside the group. We were "grinding our own axes."

A. RESPONSIBLE PARTICIPATION
was present. We were sensitive to the needs of our group. Every-one was "on the inside" par-ticipating.

1   2   3   4   5   6   7

B. LEADERSHIP
was dominated by one or more persons.

B. LEADERSHIP
was shared among the members according to their abilities and insights.

---

* This checklist may be reproduced without permission by local churches for use in their small group meetings.

C. COMMUNICATION OF IDEAS
was poor, we did not listen. We did not understand. Ideas were ignored.

1 2 3 4 5 6 7

C. COMMUNICATION OF IDEAS
was good. We listened and understood one another's ideas. Ideas were vigorously presented and acknowledged.

D. COMMUNICATION OF FEELINGS
was poor. We did not listen and did not understand feelings. No one cared about feelings.

1 2 3 4 5 6 7

D. COMMUNICATION OF FEELINGS
was good. We listened and understood and recognized feelings. Feelings were shared and accepted.

E. AUTHENTICITY
was missing. We were wearing masks. We were being phony and acting parts. We were hiding our real selves.

1 2 3 4 5 6 7

E. AUTHENTICITY
was present. We were revealing our honest selves. We were engaged in authentic self-revelation.

F. ACCEPTANCE OF PERSONS
was missing. Persons were rejected, ignored, or criticized.

1 2 3 4 5 6 7

F. ACCEPTANCE OF PERSONS
was an active part of our give-and-take. We "received one another in Christ," recognizing and respecting the uniqueness of each person.

51

G. FREEDOM OF PERSONS
was stifled. Conformity was explicitly or implicitly fostered. Persons were not free to express their individuality. They were manipulated.

1 2 3 4 5 6 7

G. FREEDOM OF PERSONS
was enhanced and encouraged. The creativity and individuality of persons was respected.

H. CLIMATE OF RELATIONSHIP
was one of hostility or suspicion or politeness or fear or anxiety or superficiality.

1 2 3 4 5 6 7

H. CLIMATE OF RELATIONSHIP
was one of mutual trust in which evidence of love for one another was apparent. The atmosphere was friendly and relaxed.

I. PRODUCTIVITY
was low. We were proud, fat, and happy, just coasting along. Our meeting was irrelevant; there was no apparent agreement.

1 2 3 4 5 6 7

I. PRODUCTIVITY
was high. We were digging hard and were earnestly at work on a task. We created and achieved something.

improving the process of your meetings, evaluation will become as much a part of your meeting as an agenda is. It will not be a wooden exercise, a thing-to-be-done before you can go home; it will be an experience in the "increase of love among men." To do without it would leave the members feeling that the meeting was unfinished.

If your group has decided to use a checklist to help in its evaluation, here is one way to go about it. At the time agreed upon (remember to allow forty-five minutes), distribute a copy of the checklist to each person in the meeting. Ask everyone to check the nine scales on the basis of how he feels about the meeting. For example, if a person feels that "responsible participation" was lacking completely, he should check 1. If he feels that everyone was really "on the inside," sharing responsibility, he should check 7. If he views responsible participation during the meeting as falling somewhere in between, he should check the appropriate number. Members are asked to check the list anonymously to allow for an expression of honest feelings.

After everyone has checked the list, gather up the papers and redistribute them. Give each person someone else's paper. The group is then asked to tabulate the ratings, each person recording on the given checklist the totals for each of the nine scales. When the members are finished with that, every person will have a profile of how the group evaluated the meeting.

Invariably, the summary of ratings shows a wide range of opinion. Members seldom agree about what went on at a meeting, and they are usually surprised to discover that not everyone saw the meeting in the same way. This divergence of feeling and opinion generally sparks a lively discussion. With the ratings before them, the members of the group have plenty of material to use in discussing how they handled content, process, and responsibility.

An evaluation of a meeting is an honest look at what the members have done, in tackling the business before them and in relating to one another. No person has all the truth about these two matters; even a majority opinion does not necessarily make one judgment right and another one wrong. All honest expressions of feeling count here; none is less important than another. Being of equal value in the eyes of God and equally responsible for doing his will, we must surely be equally worthful and responsible in the eyes of one another.

Members may question certain phrases in the checklist. People always do, and rightly so. In the first place, it is difficult to make ideas clear in short phrases; in the second place, it is difficult to make a judgment on a seven-point scale; and in the third place, the complexity of a group cannot be fully captured on paper. Nevertheless, faulty as it is, the checklist will provide a beginning for any group seeking help in evaluation. It sets out for the group's consideration much of the content, process, and responsibility aspects of group life that are discussed in this book. The use of the checklist should help members understand this book, and an understanding of this book should make more valuable the use of the checklist.

If your group is out of sorts with the checklist you have used, create another one. There is nothing sacred about a checklist. It is a tool designed to help a group improve its life and productivity, nothing more. Tools can always be improved. If you do not know how to improve your checklist, you may wish to try a different method of evaluation.

Using a person as an observer of your meeting is a different way to evaluate the functioning of your group. An observer is a group member who withdraws from the discussion for the purpose of noting and recording how the group operates. He writes down what he observes about how the group provides for content and process, and how it takes responsibility. When it is appropriate and helpful to do so, he shares what he has observed with the group.

An observer is something of a guardian or a historian of

group life. Because he is not involved in the content or the work of the group, he is free to watch how the others get the work done. Because he is not required to be critical of ideas, he is free to be sensitive to feelings. The observer is not a secretary keeping a record of the business accomplished by the group. His responsibility to the group is different from that of the other members; he helps the group see itself. When the group calls on him to lead in evaluation, he becomes a resource person, one who has evidence on paper of what happened in the meeting and how it happened.

It is not easy to be a good group observer. So much happens so fast, it is hard to keep track of it all. It simply is impossible to write it all down and then read it back. Observations, to be helpful, must be organized around a major idea. I suggest that you—or your group observer—begin with the checklist given previously in this chapter. Instead of trying to make notes and gather data about all nine categories, choose two. You might take *Responsible Participation* and *Leadership*. As you watch and listen, make notes that will help you recall for the group what patterns of leadership and participation developed.

At successive meetings you may want to use other categories for organizing your observations. After a group has become aware of some of its weaknesses and strengths, it may instruct its observer to watch particularly for certain things and perhaps even to interrupt the meeting with his observations as he makes them.

Being an observer for a group is so much fun and so helpful in learning about the dynamics of group life that the opportunity should be passed around. The most difficult part of the job is learning how to share your observations with the group.

It does not take much imagination to see that the observer could be more harmful to group morale than helpful. It is not a good thing for an observer to pass judgment

("This meeting was a failure"), to fix blame ("John's story got you off the track and you never got back"), to criticize participation, or to point a finger at particular group members. Reporting observations in any of these ways destroys trust between members of a group and arouses defenses. In fact, some groups defend themselves against a hapless but well-meaning observer by denying his judgments and questioning the accuracy of his notes.

Because one man's observations—even when observing is the only task he has to do as a group member—are always affected by his values and his perspective, an observer cannot be dogmatic about what he has seen and heard and understood. His job is probably best performed when he raises for discussion the questions about the group's life and activity that seem most pertinent to the meeting. He is expected to cite his observations that gave rise to the questions he puts before the group. But it is not his task to diagnose the disease and prescribe the cure in any but a most tentative way.

There is no right method for evaluation. In learning about Christian group life, you will probably benefit by exploring all three methods of evaluation described here. It does not matter so much *how* you do it. It matters greatly *that* you do it. An experience of love, trust, understanding, and forgiveness awaits all the hardworking and devoted members of church boards, committees, fellowship units, and study groups. They can experience a new and rewarding relationship within the fellowship of their small groups. But someone must lead the way.

THE REFORMATION CONTINUES

Evaluation is not a gimmick extraneous to the purposes of the church; on the contrary, evaluation is one means by which the church can be true to its heritage. This is especially true for Protestant Christians, who believe that no man, no clergyman, no church, and no group within the church is infallible. No traditions, no doctrines, no Bible translations, no economic or social or cultural systems are perfect and unchangeable. In fact, the opposite is true. All the activity of men and women (laymen and clergy), all the practices of the church, and all the habits and customs of our daily lives are forever in need of reform and renewal.

It is not hard for Protestants to admit that. The conviction that nothing is so good that it cannot be improved is bred in the bones of most Americans. An attitude that all things—no matter how good—must constantly be examined in the light of God's will is also bred in the fiber of Protestant Christianity.

In fact, one of the hard things about being Protestant is that you can never afford to have a closed mind on any issue. The moment you become *completely sure* that your knowledge is God's truth and that your cause or your party is God's right hand at work, at that moment you cease to follow a basic Protestant principle. Then you no longer feel the need for a living God, for you assume that you know his truth and his ways. In proclaiming the truth you know and in serving the cause you favor without a breath of a prayer for wisdom or guidance or the slightest regret for error and neglect, you become an idolator. You have placed other gods before God. You are treating the little bit of truth you know as if it were all the truth that can be known.

Protestants believe that no man, not even a denominational president or moderator chosen by the ordained leaders of the church, no Bible translation, not even the Authorized Version (King James Version) or the Revised Standard Version, no denomination (not even theirs), no political system (not even a democracy) is fully and completely an expression of God's will on earth.

This conviction, which Paul Tillich calls the Protestant principle,[7] was the basis of Luther's objections to his church. On this principle he stood, and the church was reformed.

On this principle Protestants still stand, and the church continues to be reformed.

Large and high-sounding principles, however, if they are to be effective guides to behavior, must get down to work in day-to-day existence. If they do not, they are useless and die. One place we can make this Protestant principle operative is in the evaluation aspect of our meetings. When we turn to evaluation we admit that this was not the best of all meetings, that it very likely fell short of God's will for our individual lives and for this church, and we seek to make amends for our failures and to discover better ways of working together in his service. Honest evaluation requires trust, humility, and repentance—none of which are easy attitudes of mind to achieve.

Evaluation of our group life is for Protestants not merely permissive; it is absolutely necessary. It will cost us something—our pride, our position, our advantage; but it will gain us a great deal. We will become increasingly responsible participants as we reflect upon each meeting. As we talk about how well or how poorly we handled content, process, and responsibility, we will learn how to share in the work of the church.

As Protestants we cannot be so sure of how we are working together in our churches that we cease to evaluate how we are acting in our life together. The unexamined group life is not worth living.

VI

THE LEADER
BECOMES A SERVANT

Every meeting we attend has a leader. He may be elected, appointed, or even cajoled into the job. Some leaders are skilled; others are unskilled. But most leaders are betwixt and between. Whatever the leader is, we react to his leadership. After the meeting we judge his personality, his skills, what he got done, and how long it took. In general, the judgment is unfair. As mentioned previously in chapter 3, no single person, not even the one called the leader, is alone responsible for what happens in a meeting.

WHAT IS LEADERSHIP?

Leadership is a matter of doing what is necessary for the group's functioning. It may be providing needed information, clarifying a point of view, summarizing a discussion, or any other activity that will maintain or enhance the four systems discussed in the previous chapters. At any particular time, anyone in the group can function as the leader. At various times, different persons will provide the leadership. *Leadership resides in a function, not in a person.* To be sure, during the life of a group the designated leader (the minister or chairman, for example) may perform more of these functions than anyone else because he knows more or is more concerned. But one person need not—indeed cannot—perform all the functions necessary for efficient, productive group life.

Both ordained and unordained leaders in our churches have been confused about leadership for a long time. On the one hand, church leaders have repeatedly asked members to take their rightful responsibility for witness in the world. On the other hand, church leaders, leading all kinds of groups from committee meetings to Bible study groups, frustrate the beginnings of the witness that members can make in those groups. With the best intentions in the world, church leaders have often neglected to nurture skills of ministry in the most obvious places of all: the personal relationships of small groups.

This is similar to the father who, forever urging the members of his family to learn to drive the car themselves, always insists that he knows the best way to go, how long it will take, what to take along, and what to avoid—and who invariably ends up behind the wheel himself. The family finally decides that father does not really want its members to learn how to drive. He knows how to drive well and he enjoys driving. Everyone is quite dependent upon him, and he enjoys that too. So mother and the young people relax. Let father do it, they say.

In a similar manner, church leaders have often frustrated the development of members. Leading a group in such a way as to engage the members in responsible participation requires more of a leader than does getting through an agenda on time. It is often easier for the leader to do it all himself. However, the leader who understands and is convinced about the priesthood of *all* believers will not try to run a meeting by himself. He will allow the members—maybe even wait for them—to take a responsible part. To him the quality of life present in the small group is more important than a tidy wrap-up of the business.

We Are Called to Be Servants

We have a biblical image for leadership which we have not practiced sufficiently in our churches: that of *servant.* The servant image is described in several places in the New Testament, nowhere more forcefully or more relevantly for our concern about leadership than in Luke 22:24-27:

> A dispute also arose among them, which of them was to be regarded as the greatest. And he said to them, "The kings of the Gentiles exercise lordship over them; and those in authority over them are called benefactors. But not so with you; rather let the greatest among you become as the youngest, and the leader as one who serves. For which is the greater, one who sits at table, or one who serves? Is it not the one who sits at table? But I am among you as one who serves."

Such a vision of the leader may be disturbing to our organizational-minded church today. When the church patterns much of its structure after the manner of business, government, and the military, it is easy for its members to lose sight of the servant image for leadership functions. Though we give lip service to this call of the gospel, we often act out our leadership in a different manner. But the gospel is insistent and the servant image appears again and again (for example, in Galatians 5:13-15; 1 Peter 2:16; 4:8-11; and Philippians 2:5-11).

The idea of a leader who is a servant was just as much

of an affront and puzzlement to the disciples as it is to us. In John 13:8 we read of the foot-washing episode in which Peter was embarrassed by Jesus' acting as a servant and proposing to wash Peter's feet. Peter objected strenuously. Jesus reminded his disciples, "If I then, your Lord and Teacher, have washed your feet, you also ought to wash one another's feet" (John 13:14). Service (*diakonia* is the New Testament term) is at the heart of the gospel; it begins in the humble things we do for one another.

Again and again the New Testament returns to the servant theme. It is central to Christ's own life as he gives himself to the brethren and to all mankind. Mark records that Jesus put it this way, "For the Son of man also came not to be served but to serve, and to give his life as a ransom for many" (Mark 10:45).

We can see some of the implications of the servant image for the kind of leadership described here when we think of the service that takes place around a dinner table. The host fills the plates and passes them down the table. The guests pass them to each other. At a dinner party there is no true mutuality unless everybody cooperates to keep the food moving. The success of the meal depends upon this active exchange of service that makes certain that everyone is properly fed and cared for.

The guests would be embarrassed at a dinner party if the host jumped up and down, darted around the table, and generally acted as though only he could serve them, refusing to allow them to pass dishes among themselves. They would feel like babes who were not trusted to share the responsibility for serving one another. They would probably resent such odd behavior on the part of the host, but they would submit and conform.

With the best intentions, too many church leaders have acted like such a host. They have complained about the lack of responsibility in church members, but they have gone ahead and performed most of the services themselves. The mutuality of the dinner table breaks down when one member refuses to serve another or when the host does not encourage and enable the members to serve one another. *The mutuality of the church meeting* breaks down when one member refuses to serve another or when the leader does not encourage and enable the members to serve one another.

Within the church we are called to be servant leaders. Too strong and radical an idea? The world church layman Hendrik Kraemer says that theologians, ministers, and laity "need to place their task and vocation under the light of that profound, revolutionary word: *diakonia* [service], which is not a merely ethical, humanitarian category but rather the deepest religious category, which lies at the bottom of the gospel."[8] We are concerned that this "deepest religious category" become an accurate description of *the leaders and the members* of our small group meetings. All are called to be servants. "Laity" and "ministers" do not describe two separate New Testament groups. Both words refer to all of the people, the people of God. Every Christian is called to *diakonia*. He is expected to serve and to share the ministry. In the New Testament community, every Christian was by that fact a "minister." That is still true today—and it ought to be realized more generally in the church than it actually is.

How Does a Servant-Leader Act?

1. *The servant-leader demonstrates his commitment to a shared ministry.* The crucial person in this radical recovery of shared ministry is the person presently designated as the leader. Only as he is convinced that he wants to share responsibility will he begin to act in the group in ways that will enable the members to be responsible. He expects the members to take their rightful responsibility. He knows that a shared ministry will not be accomplished overnight. But he knows the direction in which he feels impelled to move.

He knows that every group is found somewhere along the

line drawn below. On the left the leader is responsible. On the right all are responsible.

Designated leader	*Group members (including leader)*
is responsible	are responsible
provides resources	provide resources
evaluates	evaluate
provides strategies	provide strategies
communicates	communicate
listens	listen
trusts	trust

In practice probably no group can be described at either extreme. The leader who is a servant acts in ways that will enable the group to move more and more toward the right. He insists that decisions be responsible choices of all members.

2. *The servant-leader provides for all of the necessary processes of a fully functioning meeting.* But he is constantly alert, ready for the time when members begin performing some of these processes themselves. He makes certain that the necessary strategies are present. If the members are not testing, summarizing, clarifying, or perfoming a needed strategy, then he performs these functions. If the members are not communicating, then he makes certain that all of the communication process is functioning: expression, listening, and response. He trusts the members. He believes in the members. He expects them to enter into group relationship with him.

The servant-leader's performance of the processes necessary for the life of the group is temporary. He knows that the group will respond in kind, sooner or later. When it does, he will stop performing the needful function. Seeing a leader perform a strategy or function necessary for Christian group life teaches the members how to do it. For example, his listening will evoke listening in the members.

"We love because he first loved us." We listen because we have first been listened to.

3. *The servant-leader gives freely of his resources.* His knowledge, experience, and skills are readily available to the group; but he is careful not to overwhelm the group with his resources. He tries to provide these resources when they will be of genuine service to the group and its task; he does not unload his resources just because he has them. He knows that the group's needs in the beginning are more likely to be process needs of strategy, skill in communication, and the development of a climate of trust rather than needs for resources. His primary objective, always, is to serve the group's needs.

When he shares his resources, he tells not only what he knows about a subject but also how he has experienced it; not only his impersonal observations but also his personal struggle; not only his ideas but also his feelings. In other words, he shares himself. A leader who is free to disclose appropriate personal experiences is one of the most valuable resources any group can have.

4. *The servant-leader encourages evaluation.* He understands himself and exercises a personal security that allows him to accept and participate in evaluation of programs and groups. He strives to live under the Protestant principle. No present formulation of group life, program, or relationships is sacred. It can be changed. Undoubtedly it will be changed. The servant-leader encourages and participates in evaluation leading to change that improves and enhances the work of a group. In so doing, he shows himself to be a person open to change.

5. *The servant-leader practices what he preaches.* He conscientiously seeks to act as he intends, to do what he says, to practice what he preaches. Talking about the love of God and the love of neighbor, he strives to extend love in his relationships. Hearing and believing that "the people

of God have one ministry," he acts in a small group in ways designed to share that ministry with people. Knowing about the koinonia of the New Testament, he acts out his present ability to live such a life of loving relationship. Advocating forgiveness, he is forgiving and he seeks forgiveness. He strives to act out whatever he talks out. Sometimes he fails. But his intentions are clear and he keeps trying.

6. *The servant-leader is honest and trustworthy.* Whatever pressures are upon him, he shares with the group. If he is so pressed that he must hurry the usual process, he says so. If he has, for any reason, committed the group to a point of view or a program of action, he says so. If he asks for discussion and suggestions for action, he is prepared to accept the decision of the group. He does not give freedom in appearance only and then manipulate the group so that it accepts the decision he has already made.

* * *

Here are a few questions by which a leader who is trying to be a servant can judge the degree to which the members of a group are responsibly sharing in a ministry. When the leader is absent from a meeting:

1. Can the members make real and binding decisions?

2. Is prayer eliminated because only the leader can pray?

3. Is the meeting canceled because nothing can be done without the leader?

The behavior and responsibility of the members when the servant-leader is absent provides an important clue to the nature and degree of shared ministry that is actually present.

OTHER LEADERSHIP CONSIDERATIONS

Ideal leadership permits all members to play responsible roles in the group's functioning. This is particularly true in

Christian group life. Here each person becomes a responsible participant in the meeting. Mature relationships and productive work emerge from such meetings. But leadership that has such happy consequences is not easy to generate. With certain groups or in certain situations, even the best servant-leadership will call forth no more than meager results. The leader who works at his task becomes aware in time of these additional considerations.

1. *Characteristics of the group may make a difference.* The previous experience of the members affects their readiness and their ability to take a responsible part in the work of their group and of the church.

A large church called a new minister. At the December deacons' meeting he asked for comments about previous lenten programs and suggestions for the coming year. There was an awkward silence among the members, many of whom were responsible leaders in the community. There were no ideas advanced. Finally, one of the men asked, "Where is the mimeographed sheet?" "What sheet?" asked the new minister. The members enlightened him by saying that the previous minister always brought a mimeographed page outlining the lenten program. The members then commented and agreed to it. It took some time for the new minister to convince the deacons that he was not going to be solely responsible for making the decisions about the life of the church. Once the laymen began to feel a genuine responsibility to share the ministry, a whole new life opened up for them and the church.

The expectations of the members affect what happens in a group. Many people think of a good leader as an enthusiastic, hard-driving, highly organized person who gets things done with dispatch. In turn they think of a good member as a bright, flexible, cooperative person who follows the leader. Such a picture of leader-member behavior and relationship will stand in the way of servant-leadership and servant-membership. Until members are convinced that benevolent dictatorship (for such it is) is neither democratic nor Christian group life, they will be slow to respond to any other kind.

The age of the members is a factor in how well a group lives together and works together. The younger the group, the less experienced its members will be. However, this does not mean that an adult leader of a youth fellowship should assume responsibilities that young people can and should and really want to carry themselves. Since persons learn to be responsible by being responsible, depriving any person, aged seven or seventeen or forty-seven, of a responsibility that is his does him a disservice. The young age of the members of some groups may be more of a stumbling block for the leader than a handicap for the group.

The cultural, educational, economic, historical background of the members may make a difference. Sometimes leaders feel that only strong directive leadership will work with persons from the inner city. Those who live in the inner city have had inadequate education and limited opportunities for self-direction. Sometimes suburban leaders feel that only strong directive leadership will work with suburban people. Suburbanites are busy and accustomed to such direction. When judgments like these determine the kind of leadership exercised with either of these groups of people, the group members are stunted in their Christian growth. They are deprived of their witness to each other and of the support of each other. Even worse, the strong directive leaders become the "religious persons" who act for the others, the "experts" in the field of religion. Since no expert can make another's decisions in matters involving the love of God and the love of neighbor, here too the people have been cheated.

As with age, cultural factors may be more of an excuse for a particular style of leadership than a limiting factor in the growth of Christian group life.

2. *The setting in which the group works may make a difference.* Where a group meets, how often, how long, the nature of its business, and how it must accomplish its business may all be prescribed by the by-laws of a church. Some of these conditions will impose restrictions on certain groups. For example, a group that must proceed by Robert's *Rules of Order* may find it difficult to improve the process of its meeting and to profit from an evaluation. A group that meets only two hours once a month may find it difficult to build a climate of trust in which responsibility can be shared. A group that sits in rows of chairs with a leader up front will find that members have difficulty in communicating with one another.

The setting—rules for meeting, time available, physical arrangements—may make a difference to a group, but should not be used as an excuse for doing business in the same old way. The servant-leader works to eliminate or to lessen any restrictive influences of the setting upon the meeting.

3. *It matters what you believe and how you feel about people.* Whatever you believe about yourself, you must also believe about other persons. If you feel that you are a person of worth, able to be responsible, it follows that other persons also are of worth and capable of responsibility, for we are all God's children. Any discrepancy between your beliefs about yourself and about other persons frustrates servant-leadership. You cannot feel yourself responsible and at the same time feel that all other persons are irresponsible *and* become a servant-leader.

You have to believe that persons have something worth saying in order to listen and respond to them. You have to believe that people are trustworthy in order to trust them enough to share responsibility with them.

Most groups, leaders and members, can do a better job than they are now doing. Most groups will do a better job as soon as a leader, or a member, points the way.

VII

THE MEMBER
BECOMES A SERVANT

A good servant gives himself to others without being preoccupied with himself, his own prestige, or his own desires. A responsible group member gives himself to the work and the life of the group without being preoccupied with himself, his own prestige, or his own desires. As servants, members are called to share in the maintenance of the systems of the group—content, process, responsibility, and evaluation—along with the servant-leader.

How does an ordinary member of a group become a servant-member? What does he say, what does he do, how does he serve?

1. *A servant-member contributes both ideas and feelings to the meeting.*

2. *A servant-member is sensitive to others' ideas and feelings in the meeting.*

We are quite used to dealing with words and ideas. We are not so skilled in dealing with feelings. In fact, we often do not recognize that feelings underlie the words that a member speaks in our meetings. Sometimes the feelings are strong and clear, sometimes they are tentative and vague; but always they are present in every expression. Feelings are as much a part of the content of a meeting as words are.

If the meeting is to demonstrate Christianity at work, feelings must be expressed and accepted and included as part of the planning, discussion, and decision making.

A servant-member contributes his ideas when it is appropriate to do so. His ideas may strengthen a point of view under discussion, may clarify confusion or disagreement, may be a creative solution to a conflict of ideas and interests, or may offer a third choice. He listens and thinks and waits for the right time, the helpful moment to say what he thinks. He does not withhold the best he has to offer.

He behaves in the same way when he expresses his feelings. Far from hurling them at the group or dumping them in the middle of things, he reveals his feelings when that promises to be helpful to the group's process. He says how he feels and why. He offers his feelings for consideration by the group.

For example, in an executive board meeting considering the need for a large building program, a member reveals his need "to be a better Christian." He confesses that since joining the church he has not ministered to anyone, or learned more about Christianity, or experienced anything in his church relationships that was different from a pleasant, polite social group. He readily admits his responsibility for this condition of his soul; yet he feels that he needs some help. He would rather see the church put additional money into program and competent staff instead of into more buildings.

This member served the meeting of the executive board by honestly revealing himself. He accused no one; he sought their help. His example brought equally honest response. Many felt about themselves as he did and were sure there were others in the congregation who felt the same. At this church meeting, there was initiated a thoughtful study of what belonging to the church should mean to people and of how the programs of the church could be Christian rather than just pleasant, social events. The member in question served better than he might have imagined he would.

A servant-member not only contributes his own ideas and feelings; he hears and understands the ideas and feelings of others. If he fails to understand, he asks questions until he does. He listens with his heart. He hears what people are saying and he knows how they are feeling. He watches to see that neither ideas nor feelings are ignored. The presence of a servant-member in a group improves communication and builds trust.

3. *A servant-member helps to improve the process of a meeting.* He knows how to keep track not only of ideas and feelings but also of the process of the group's functioning. If there are many individual, unrelated ideas before the group at one time, he summarizes and clarifies and integrates the discussion. For example:

"Some people who have been members of this church for a long time think . . . ."

"Some who quite recently have come from other churches feel . . . ."

"As I understand it, Mary and John do not agree with either of these points of view. Is that right?"

If no one appears to be listening to a particular person, the servant-member listens and responds so that the speaker knows he has been heard and the group is made aware of another contribution.

If the group is faced with a situation that it finds almost impossible to cope with intelligently *and* lovingly, the servant-member tries to propose a strategy that will lead to a solution. If he cannot think of such a proposal, he calls the group's attention to its impasse and asks whether anyone can think of a way out. He initiates activity that helps the group handle its problem.

Sometimes the servant-member may have to interrupt, even stop, swift-moving conversation to make sure that a contribution has been heard and included in the group's thinking. Sometimes he may have to postpone expressing his own concerns or ideas or feelings in the interest of helping the group to deal with those already expressed.

Sometimes he may have to express his own uneasiness or dissatisfaction with accepted programs or procedures or decisions because they seem to him to be superficial or irrelevant in the light of the command to "love your God with all your heart and soul and mind and strength, and your neighbor as yourself."

The servant-member performs whatever task is necessary to serve the group, except leaving the meeting to get the coffee ready. He lets Martha do that.

4. *A servant-member may initiate evaluation.* He asks, "How are we doing?" or "Is this the most useful way for us to function?" or "I wonder what happened at that particular time in the meeting?" or "Let's look at the way in which we operated as a group tonight." The servant-member knows that the most non-threatening way to initiate evaluation is to evaluate some part of his own functioning during the meeting and to invite the other members to comment. He may begin, "I felt that I was trying to talk all of you into a point of view that apparently didn't interest you or make sense to you. Did it seem that way to you?"

At another time before the group disperses, he may seek ways of opening discussion about the way in which the meeting progressed and what the group accomplished.

The servant-member has an attitude of research about his own participation and his understanding of the process that takes place in small groups. He may keep running notes or a diary of the meetings he attends in order to profit from his own reflections. A servant-member learns how to learn from his own experience.

5. *A servant-member is personally involved: he is responsible.* How or why a person becomes personally involved in the life of the church is a matter about which no one knows everything. But we do know that a member of a group who becomes its servant is personally involved in the life of that group and of the church. He has something at stake. He rejoices in the group's accomplishments and regrets its failures. Part of his identity—who he is in his own eyes and in the eyes of his neighbors—comes from his deep involvement in the activities of his group.

There is risk in becoming deeply involved in any human relationship. Being a member of a group takes time, and thought, and talent. The servant-member knows this and freely chooses to give himself to it. He knows that in trying to be true to his convictions about his life, he will disclose himself to the other members. They will see his strengths and his weaknesses. He may wind up on the unpopular side of an issue, work hard for something that fails, or offend some other members of the church. He knows the perils; he knows also the *promise*. A man without convictions may avoid being hurt or making enemies. He also *misses* having his life count for something.

It follows that a member who is deeply involved in the life of a group feels responsible to the group and for the group. He feels an obligation to make whatever contribution he can to the work of the group. The group needs him; he will not let it down.

6. *A servant-member changes and grows as a member of the Christian community.* He is prepared to look at a situa-ation, the other members, and himself and to change his attitudes and his actions when that is necessary. He has the courage to look at his behavior and his thinking and to make adjustments in the face of continuing conflict with other members, lack of accomplishment, persistent uneasi-ness in the group, personal unhappiness, and a hypercritical attitude from others. He is able to hear the truth that others speak to him in love, to repent of his insensitivity, to seek forgiveness, and to make amends if he can.

In all these ways he seeks to increase the love of God and of neighbor as he lives and works in a small group assigned to carry out part of the work of the church.

❋   ❋   ❋

If all of these actions that describe the servant-member sound very much like the ones that describe the servant-leader, they have not been misunderstood. They are not different at all in the final analysis. A designated leader of a group has initial responsibility, which means that at first he may carry more responsibility. But a good servant seeks to serve to the limit of his ability and understanding, no matter whether he is a servant-leader or a servant-member.

VIII

A SMALL GROUP
AT WORK

Every person, sometime in his life, thinks about changes he would like to make in himself. He would like to be more outgoing to others, more adequate in his job, more loving in his family, more responsible in his community, more thoughtful of others, less preoccupied with himself.

Jesus knew of this yearning for change deep within every person, and much of his ministry was spent in helping people to change. True to her Lord, the church too has been committed to the task of helping people to change. However, the church has not known for certain how people change and when and why. No one knows really. Change is a difficult thing to observe, particularly in persons. Even the person who has changed seldom knows all the circumstances that made his change possible.

But more is known about how people change than the church puts into conscious practice. Very little change occurs in a person who is simply told to be different (there go the sermons!). Most change occurs in the person who becomes deeply involved in a community that lives the kind of changed life to which he aspires (here come the small groups!).

Let us look at one man's experience in a small group and see what clues it offers us for our small groups in the church.

THE BIBLE STUDY GROUP

After some hesitation, Baird Thompson and his wife joined a Bible study group in their local church. The group was composed of six couples, including the minister and his wife. A salesman in his late thirties, Baird was comfortably successful. He and his wife and their three children lived in a pleasant neighborhood. But the outward appearance of contentment did not always correspond to Baird's inner feeling. Business was competitive and rough. Uncertainty about his future sometimes made him anxious. There were disharmonious things in Baird's life that troubled him. He joined the Bible study group with an unspoken hope that he would find something that would enable him to be different.

One of the things that made Baird uneasy about the Bible study group was the opening prayer. For the first several meetings it was offered by the minister. Baird realized that this was the customary way to begin church meetings. He was not really opposed to prayer, but in his own life he was very puzzled about the meaning of prayer. However, he went along with the group. There was not much else he could do. At the fourth meeting, one of the members said to the group, "I'm afraid I must confess that the opening prayer does not have much meaning for me." Baird was startled by this honesty and wondered what would happen. To his amazement everyone, including the minister, listened to this viewpoint without condemnation. Here began the most remarkable hour-and-a-half that Baird had ever experienced in a church group. Everyone talked honestly about his experience with prayer. For some, prayer was obviously a most meaningful and important part of the daily routine. For others, like Baird, it represented something they felt they ought to do and yet did not do. One person flatly said that prayer had no meaning for him, though he did find value in meditation, which he felt was a kind of prayer. As a result of the long discussion, the group decided upon a method of starting each meeting by which the responsibility for the beginning would be rotated. The decision for silence, meditation, or prayer was to be made by the member responsible for the particular meeting. By the time the evening was over, everyone had new ideas about prayer and a greatly increased respect for the other members.

Shortly after the prayer discussion, Baird faced an important decision in his life. Another firm had offered him a job as sales manager. The job would mean only a small increase in salary but a significant increase in prestige. Baird was intrigued but fearful of the new job offer. He was not sure he could handle it. If he could not, he would be worse off than if he had never made the change from salesman.

He did not tell the group about the offer. He talked with some of his fellow salesmen, with a couple of friends in the community, and even with two of his customers. He came away from these conversations very much discouraged because these people did not seem to understand the real dilemma he faced in this decision. Each of them had a quick solution. It all added up to: *Take the job.* Even Baird's wife did not seem to understand his misgivings about his ability. To whom could he talk about such personal feelings?

One night at the Bible study meeting Baird mentioned the choice he was facing. Some of the members quickly sensed the importance of his decision. They carefully listened to Baird as no one else had done. They clarified his ideas and his feelings. One of the men volunteered to talk again with Baird and to provide some further information for him. When the meeting was over, Baird had a new feeling about himself and about the group. He had been treated as a person of worth. His anxiety about whether he could handle the new job was understood and respected. He felt that the people of that Bible study group, which he had joined so reluctantly, sincerely cared for him. He was deeply appreciative.

Baird's retired parents always came for a three-week visit sometime during the year. Prior to and during these visits Baird was edgy. It was all he could do to hold his tongue and tolerate the demands that his parents placed upon the household. In the Bible study meeting before the arrival of his parents, Baird's edginess and anger spilled out. His wife tried to hush him up but he silenced her. To his new-found friends he told an emotional and bitter tale of a restricted childhood and rebellious adolescence. The annual parental visit had been a bone of contention between Baird and his wife since their marriage. She felt that he was making too much of minor and long-past events. He felt that she was minimizing his experiences. They had long since declared an armed truce. They did not talk about the matter; they endured it.

The group listened thoughtfully. The members did not condemn Baird for his hostility toward his parents, and he began to feel less defensive and less angry. His fellow members tried to understand the problem as Baird saw it. During the discussion his wife made several suggestions. When he began to argue with her, members of the group intervened, "Baird, you are not listening to your wife." Chagrined, he stopped talking and began listening. The group slowly helped Baird and his wife to communicate with each other for the first time in years about this issue of the parents. A painful breach in their relationship began to heal and the chance of a new relationship with his parents was made possible because of his experiences that night.

Toward the end of the year, the Bible study group and other members of the church were asked to meet with a group of seminary students in training for the ministry. After dinner the students and the church members paired off to talk individually. The seminarians wanted to learn firsthand about the ideas, convictions, and witness of laymen. Baird found himself talking for an hour and a half with an earnest young man. Baird heard himself explaining how it was to try to live a Christian life in the business world, what it meant to study scripture, what prayer meant to him, and how he had actually changed in recent months. Baird talked about his own religious experience; he listened to the student's doubts and hopes. In his struggle to communicate with the student, Baird realized how different he himself was because of his belonging to the Bible study group during the past year.

CONDITIONS OF CHANGE

Baird's experience with the Bible study group illustrates several of the conditions which, when they are present in a group, enable persons to change, to overcome their estrangements, to live more adequate lives, to do what is Christian. As we consider groups to which we belong, we need to ask about the extent to which one or more of these conditions are present.

1. *If a group offers significant new belonging to a member, he may become a different person, a "new being."* To the extent that a person genuinely accepts membership in a group, he also accepts the values and beliefs of that group. Baird slowly found himself "belonging" to the Bible study group and accepting its values. The new belonging became more important and meaningful than his other "belongings." The new belonging enabled Baird to change.

We see this condition for change in many life situations. The adolescent gives up some or all of his family belonging to find a new belonging in the teen-age culture. Sometimes the young person changes his appearance as well as his values in order to be a part of the new group. He is, in fact, reeducated by an intensive new we-feeling. Unfortunately, church youth groups have seldom provided significant new belonging for teen-agers. But whenever they have, as in a work camp or in a summer conference, change has usually occurred.

Alcoholics Anonymous is a group that practices all six of the conditions of change described in this section and that knows the importance of a new belonging for the alcoholic. When he accepts A. A. membership, when he is committed to the Twelve Steps of A. A., when he feels and hears and receives understanding and help and service from fellow A. A.'s who owe him nothing and to whom he owes more than he can repay, an alcoholic finds an important new belonging for his life. If he accepts the new belonging, he may conquer his alcoholism; if he rejects it, he is likely to bring total disaster to himself and to all who have lived and worked with him.

The changes in their lives indicate that the disciples who followed Jesus accepted a new belonging. They gave up their previous belongings to families, fishermen, and tax collectors as they felt an increasing identification with Jesus and with one another. Belonging to the group known as the disciples of Jesus slowly became the most significant relationship of their lives. After the events of the death and resurrection of Jesus, the disciples were left alone. The extent to which this new belonging had become all important for them became evident in the strength of their witness and in the maintenance of their common life, even against the social and religious patterns of their culture. They had changed. They were followers of "the way."

The changes that come because of a new belonging are

lasting only when they have been freely accepted by the member. Questions and doubts must be dealt with and a new way of life must be made real. Coercion may lead to a temporary new belonging and the apparent acceptance of new values, but sooner or later the power that coerces disappears. If the disciples had been coerced into following Jesus, they would not have continued in the faith after Jesus departed from them. The alcoholic who is coerced into attending A. A. meetings will backslide when the coercive force is removed unless he has come to accept the new belonging with enthusiasm. The boy who is coerced into attending a church school class is not likely to remain after the coercion is removed.

Too many of our churches and the groups within them provide only secondary belongings for the members. Sitting in a pew on a Sunday morning is not likely to produce a radical new belonging. Church members find their primary belonging some other place. When pressed, the member lives up to the values and beliefs of those "other places." Whenever the church has been a transforming power for individuals and for their culture, it has been the center of a radical new belonging for its members.

2. *If a group offers support and understanding to a member facing crisis, he can change.* In a crisis a person is faced with sudden decisions and choices. He often does not know what to do. He may fear that he does not have the resources to weather the crisis. A supporting group enables a person to face his crisis with less panic and greater objectivity. When Baird shared the crisis of a job decision with the group, he was able to share his fears within a supporting community. Baird was free to face his anxieties and the group was free to help.

Crises come to churches as well as to individual persons. A young minister committed to a racially integrated church worked toward this goal for eight years in his preaching, his pastoral work, and in the educational activities of the church he served. Creative and significant programs in family camps, the youth group, and several study groups explored the meaning of Christian brotherhood. Many church members visited with minority groups in the community. Negroes visited the church and were welcomed to the worship service and to other activities. The logical and inevitable happened. A young Negro couple asked to join the church. To the amazement of many, the membership split down the middle when faced with this decision.

In the midst of one of the many long discussions, a member in favor of integration turned to the opposition and asked, "How could you have listened to our minister's preaching and participated in all of the activities of this church for eight years and then vote against this couple's admission?"

The answer came quickly, "Oh, it was all right as long as the minister only preached about social justice. Taking this couple into membership is a completely different matter."

Church groups need to welcome crisis and to face it directly, for decision making reveals our weaknesses and our strengths as a people of God. Living without crises may seem more appealing, but it is pretty lukewarm living and it does not count for much in a world of hurt and injustice.

> "And to the angel of the church in Laodicea write: . . . . 'I know your works: you are neither cold nor hot. Would that you were cold or hot! So, because you are lukewarm, and neither cold nor hot, I will spew you out of my mouth'" (Rev. 3:14-16).

3. *If the persons in a group speak honestly about themselves, a person can change.* During a summer conference, the effects of honest speaking were experienced in an unexpected way. Each morning's session consisted of an address followed by a small group discussion of one and one-

half hours. The lectures were interpretations of the relevance of the gospel to the needs of men.

In one of these small groups, polite discussion of the lecture followed the first meeting. One did not have to listen long to know that the talk was at a superficial level, however. The second meeting was the same. Midway through the third day a member said, "I have the overwhelming feeling that not one of us, myself included, has been talking about anything very important as yet. Maybe I am wrong, but it just seems to me that in our limited time this week I ought to be honest with the group about my own feelings and behavior at this point."

The unimportant conversations ceased. Every member looked first at the speaker and then into space. After a full minute-and-a-half silence during which time the person who had spoken looked increasingly uncomfortable, another member spoke. In an entirely different tone of voice from the one she had used during the previous two-and-a-half days she said, "You're right and I'm glad you had the courage to be so honest. When I go home from this conference, I face a major decision in my family. I have hardly been able to think of anything else, but it scarcely seemed proper to bring up such an intensely personal concern in a beautiful conference setting. You have given me the opportunity and I must share my problem with you because maybe you can help."

From that time on the meetings became an interchange of Christian concern and testimony. Long after the conference was over, the members recalled their common experience with great appreciation. Without the practice of honesty on the part of one member, the real hopes of the conference would not have been realized for that small group. Superficiality would have remained the order of the day.

Practicing honesty in a group is tempting and threatening at the same time. We know that we cannot be transformed if we keep hiding our real feelings and ideas; besides we misgivings and their convictions. To Baird's surprise he discovered one day that he was interpreting some of his own experiences in the light of a biblical concept that he had become aware of only recently. He had found a new interpretation of existence, a Christian one, which had changed both his understanding of and his attitude toward the events of his own life.

6. *If a group provides for an experiencing of the Christian life, a member can become a different person.* Experiencing is the tryout of new ways of behaving, the actual acting out of new interpretations. To change, a person needs to *do* as well as to *discuss*. In Baird's dialogue with the seminarian, he was witnessing to his own Christian experiences.

Another illustration is found in the Bible study group's discussion and decision about the opening prayer. As each member took his turn in beginning the meeting with meditation, silence, or prayer, he was no longer dealing with explanations about prayer. He was experiencing prayer or meditation or silence in a new way. On Baird's second turn, much to his surprise, he concluded the silence not with a mere amen but with a brief and hesitant but obviously sincere prayer. Out of that initial experiencing, Baird subsequently felt able to offer prayer at committee meetings in the church and at the table in his own home.

Experiencing the Christian life is one reason work camps are so successful in the transformation of young people. The work camp automatically provides this condition of change when the members begin to serve people through their work. They live a life of concern and ministry as they lead a vacation church school, build a community playground, repair or rehabilitate houses or schools, construct irrigation ditches, or carry through any of a dozen other projects. Because they have experienced Christian ministry, they know what it is all about and they believe in it.

Churches offer far too little experiencing of the Christian

want to be known as we are. At the same time we are fearful. Will the others still want us around if we say honestly what we think and feel? Will we be acceptable if we reveal our true selves? It takes courage to be honest, but it takes a great amount of energy to maintain a dishonest position or a facade.

Baird's first experience in the Bible study group—when members of the group honestly discussed their feelings about prayer—convinced him that he could express his true feelings to these people and trust them to accept him. He discovered that honest self-disclosure was characteristic of the relationship of these people to each other. Had Baird not believed this, he would not have told the group of his job decision or of his anguish about his relationship to his parents.

4. *If a group provides for the healing of relationships, a person can change.* Whenever a person is feeling bad about himself or about someone else (the two feelings almost always exist together), he is estranged and he is in need of reconciliation. That is, he needs to be restored to community, to relationship, to wholeness. He needs to experience a sense of his own worth and acceptability. He needs to forgive and to be forgiven, to love and to be loved, to understand and to be understood, to listen and to be heard.

The anxious, worried, bitter, nagging, driving, withdrawn persons among us are suffering persons. They are at war with themselves. The violent battle raging deep within demands so much energy and attention that they appear to be indifferent to other people. They are estranged from themselves.

Others among us are estranged from their families, their colleagues, their neighbors, or their friends. A breakdown in trust or communication between people who live and work together is a regrettable and unhappy experience. It cries to be put aside, to be forgiven and forgotten. No one wants to live in disharmony with others, feeling hurt, peevish, envious, or slighted. Nursing these feelings and protecting oneself against further misuse by others requires so much psychic energy that there is little left for loving, rejoicing, caring, helping, and creating. It is hard to think of anyone else when you are hard at work caring for yourself.

Finding oneself in the midst of a community that loves without condemning is the beginning of the end of estrangement. Jesus offered his love and concern in the name of God to all people, even to those whom his community called sinners. By that act the most despised were restored to lives of mercy and loving-kindness. We who are members of the Christian church, the Body of Christ on earth today, must offer our love and concern in his name to all people, especially to those who are at sixes and sevens with themselves and others. In no other way can a man or woman believe again in his own worth and love God's gift of life.

The beginning of the healing of Baird's estrangement from his parents and the restoration of communication between him and his wife began with the group's thoughtful listening to his story. Acted out in that meeting were the words, "Neither do I condemn you; go, and do not sin again" (John 8:11b). Baird's behavior and interpretations were not approved; neither was he condemned. The Bible study group knew him at his worst and continued to care for him. In that group relationship, Baird found insight and new encouragement for working at his estrangements and changing his relationships to those around him.

5. *If a group provides a new interpretation of existence, a member can become a different person.* Man lives in a world of meanings. This world of meanings is an idea structure that helps him make sense out of his world, that influences his decisions, and that is used in helping him understand his experiences and feelings. Baird had an inadequate interpretation of parents in general and of his relationship

to his own parents in particular. In the meeting descr earlier, a new interpretation began to emerge for B This new meaning helped make new action possible ir lation to his parents.

A new interpretation cannot be handed to a person a letter. Such a "delivery" usually fails and winds up in file of forgotten advice. Often the church in its var meetings has been guilty of assuming that because a i ister or a leader or a curriculum or a creed or a confere resolution proclaims a new interpretation of life, the m bers will be transformed. But persons do not adopt patterns of meanings so easily.

Baird is a good example. During his lifetime he had I told, he had read, and he had heard about other way relating to parents. But he had not lived by these new in pretations. If anyone had told him prior to joining the B study group that he was going to adopt a new interpreta of his relationship to his parents, he would have been sl tical. But in the Bible study group, where Baird experien reconciliation, honesty, support in a crisis, and a new longing, he did just that. He was at last able to discover adopt a new interpretation and to accept new knowle from others.

Members of Bible study groups often discover new in pretations, new meanings, and new insights into many ferent aspects of their lives through their study and disc sion of Bible passages. When each member has to wre with the passage himself, think about it, interpret it, a translate it into his own life, he experiences what it me to hear the Word of God. He may read commentaries a listen to what his minister thinks, but not until he deci what the passage means to him in terms of the life he living will he have heard the Bible speak to him.

The members of Baird's Bible study group talked hones and critically about the passages they studied and about t meaning of these passages for their lives. They shared th

life, even of prayer. A prominent minister who was asked to write a lenten devotional booklet told later of his experience. He recalled that he struggled for months to create brief meditations around biblical themes, concluding with short prayers. He agonized over the meditations and the interpretation of the biblical material. He wrote and rewrote the prayers. Finally the booklet was finished and printed. It was distributed to thousands of people who used it during Lent. Many people told the minister that it was a very good devotional booklet. But as he reflected about his experiencing of the assignment, he made the comment that *he was the one who really benefited* by the whole effort. How could anyone else have felt the intensity of preparation and of soul-searching that went into those meditations and prayers? They were that particular minister's prayers and his meditations. It was his experiencing. He was in fact transformed by the experience, for it changed his prayer life. He always wondered whether the devotional booklet had changed or transformed anyone else.

CONCLUSION

Following the teachings of her Master, Jesus Christ, the church began as a fellowship in which persons were enabled to repent and change. Many people in local congregations are looking for transformation; but when they are desperate, they seek a psychiatrist or an educator or someone outside the church. The church seems uninterested or unskilled—or both—in helping people to change. The fact that there are so many church meetings that offer so few of the conditions necessary for transformation should convince us of our need to repent and to change the way in which we have invested time spent together in small group meetings.

Transformation is the promise of the gospel and the witness of many, even today. The small group meetings of our churches can be—and should be—an experience of the life of the Christian community.

89

IX

HOW A PERSON
CHANGES IN A GROUP

When people change, they know it. Some persons, more sensitive to reflection than the rest of us, can remember the day and the hour that change began. They know what kind of day it was and what they were wearing. What is more important, they know what kind of person they were then and what kind they are becoming now.

For several years the members of a seminary course have kept diaries of their experiences in the class. The course is an effort to educate young men and women entering the ministry in the dynamics, understandings, and skills necessary to Christian group life.

The following diary (used by permission and changed

90

only to disguise the members) is an authentic, firsthand report from one of the members. It tells the story of his change
from mere membership to responsible participation in a
particular group.

First Meeting

Again, as in all first encounters with a new group, I was reti-
cent, or more bluntly, scared stiff; nerves running wild. Wondered for a while what I was doing there. Hoped that I can
overcome this habit of keeping a defensive wall up and trap shut
during the first and even subsequent group encounters. Was
deeply impressed with the potential value that this group might
have for our learning. Wished they would set a purpose for the
group so that I would feel more comfortable. Am I lazy or
scared? Must be a responsible member; will attempt to climb
over own protective wall next session.

Second Meeting

Well, here I am; don't feel too nervous this time. I felt that
it might make people more at ease if I let them know how I
felt at this point. I did, but it doesn't seem that there was really
much need for it. I am interested, but what can I say, the discussions have been very interesting so far and I still feel that
what I have to say would tend to slow or hamper. I am participating—yet can this discussion really be valuable if I don't
talk? I don't know. We will just have to see what happens,
maybe when we get off this intellectual plane and begin to
talk cases I will feel that I can participate verbally. What do I
mean by talking cases? Must clarify this for myself—soon!

Third Meeting

Unable to attend.

Fourth Meeting (apparently written during the meeting)

Yes, and actually it was a real shame that I did miss last
meeting. I am lost. They are talking about something on the
board; it is senseless. You sap, now it's too late to find out what
went on in the last meeting. Why didn't you say something? O
good, Bill seems to have sensed my need and is putting it on

the board. They seem to think that this is not a group action—is not this effort the same as or at least as valuable as a verbal response? Say it! Say it! Say, "Thank you, Bill, I was kind of lost because I could not be here last week." I did say it—but too late though!

Fifth Meeting

I am reacting in the same old way; my anger shuts me up; I just don't talk when I'm mad. Boy! John came up with an almost verbatim statement of something I had said, "You can lead me to the water, but you can't make me drink" and then proceeded to say that he was sick and tired of "intellectualisms." Why didn't I say it was how I felt and that it took the form of words to express this feeling? No, I got real mad and as usual when mad closed my mouth for the rest of the time, and how long that was. I almost spoke at the close, but everyone was packing up to leave and so did I; I have had it. Time to do something!

Sixth Meeting

This was one of the easiest sessions yet. I no longer feel the utter frustration of always being nervous. I felt that at the moment I could say something without hesitation or pressure. I have been able to get to know John much better at the meal we had together. . . . Perhaps my quietness is due to the fact that I cannot open up to a stranger; but then I must do this somehow, somewhere; for how can one get rid of the strangeness if scared, nervous, and "shut-up"? I must remember this. important for a person.

Seventh Meeting

I really don't know what induced me to speak, but perhaps it was the feeling that this group was open and accepting. I was moved by Art's honesty the week before and the way the group worked with him. This was the help I guess I was looking for. It was really a good feeling to realize that I had opened myself to the group and was actually talking. A very good evening, an evening which has proved to me that I can be an active participant.

Eighth Meeting

Unable to attend.

Ninth Meeting

Sort of felt lost after this meeting. I didn't know what to say to the question of whether or not it was a real religious experience. I felt a little guilty for not answering, but I didn't know what to say and I needed more time to think about it. The real value of the meeting in which we talked about me was in the fact that I have gained confidence and courage to face not only the personal problem but also future group encounters. Don't think I got this across. Felt sorry for Bill because I had drifted off in thought too, and when I came back to the discussion and began listening, I was lost. What were we talking about?

Tenth Meeting

It is a shame that Robert was not open to the experience of risk and encounter with the group. [For me] the group feels like a good "old shoe"—comfortable and nice.

Eleventh Meeting

Gee, this is the last meeting—never thought I would be so relaxed in a group. . . . I was relaxed, but wow, how we treated Robert. Was this fair? I think that the observations were absolutely true, but will it have any value for Robert? Can we say: "Robert, you would not let your mask down?" Or must it be a growth of insight and thus a realization on his part that he has been hiding? I guess we didn't know how to bring Robert to insight. We merely tried to feed him with it in the last few seconds of the last meeting. This will prey on my mind for a long while—it may be a lesson learned—that one must not attempt to tell a member how to act in a group, that a member can only learn this by himself. I was really uncomfortable.

I guess the greatest realization [for me] is the fact that when one goes into a group with the intense feeling that he must talk and then he doesn't, he is pushing authenticity out the window if he forces himself to talk. For me—I realize that when I have something to say, I can and will say it. This is a movement from a "nervous duty" to a comfortable desire to be a part of what is going on *either* silently *or* verbally!

Although the experiences of George Stevens, as we shall call him, are unique to him, the underlying changes revealed are basic to the changes that must take place within each one of us if we are to become adequate persons for Christian service. These changes do not foster conformity or eliminate conflict. They do enable each person increasingly to discover his uniqueness and to make his unique contribution to the church. The diary of George Stevens shows evidence of the following gradual changes or movements that he experienced.

1. *A movement from self-centeredness to care for others.* George's reflections in the first several meetings are typical of initial self-centeredness and concern about "how I am doing." In the second meeting there is some indication that he was not alone in his self-centeredness. He tried to say something, but no one seemed to care. Another member reflected on a similar experience in these words: "I feel like a flower, fighting for survival in the spring, that has been stepped on. I was trying very hard tonight but was ignored. No one responded to me—almost as if I had not been there at all. . . . I made the suggestion and no one listened. No response at all. Boy, this disturbed me! Now I want to continue what I did for the rest of this session—curl up and watch the world [go by]."

By the last meeting we find that George had moved to a concern for other persons, notably for Robert. He was no longer totally concerned about himself; he wondered how he could extend help and care to Robert. In the ninth meeting he expressed empathy and care for Bill. He had moved from focusing on himself alone to concern for other members as well.

2. *A movement from doubt about self to trust of self.* It is probably true that in the beginning of each new small

group meeting, many members have some feelings of inadequacy and some questions about their ability to participate. So long as these feelings persist, these members will hesitate to think and act creatively in the work of the group. Persons differ radically in the degree to which they possess such feelings. Sometimes this doubt about self is expressed as a feeling of worthlessness or lack of self-confidence. Of the opening session George wrote, "Wondered for a while what I was doing there." And then in the second meeting he said, "I still feel that what I have to say would tend to slow or hamper." But by the seventh meeting some of this doubt had dissipated and he had begun to trust himself by saying, "An evening which has proved to me that I can be an active participant." And in the ninth meeting he reflected about the new "confidence and courage to face not only the personal problem but also future group encounters." The record shows that something happened to George.

In the course of these sessions he had discovered that he was a person of worth and some adequacy. Such feelings about himself had a clear effect upon his ability to participate.

3. *A movement from irresponsibility to a sense of responsibility for self and others.* After the first session George Stevens wrote, "Am I lazy or scared? Must be a responsible member; will attempt to climb over own protective wall next session." He felt irresponsible both in relationship to himself and to the group. He was struggling to become a responsible member. By the tenth and eleventh meetings George felt that he, along with the others, was responsible for how the meeting went and for what the group could do for Robert.

A tendency to be irresponsible and to blame others for what is happening often leads to withdrawal from the group. A member of another small group meeting revealed this reaction:

What's the use of toying. Again and again I feel very frustrated at what is happening. What is happening? NOTHING. We just sit there spinning our wheels. I just want to quit even trying to say anything about this session. I've had just about enough of this frustration.

I've successfully withdrawn myself from the group—sealed myself off, at least, from saying anything that is important from inside my own deepest concerns. And I view the group sliding into this shallow dickering, this intellectual escape from the members' real concerns. Really, I feel now like simply ending the problem by saying, "To hell with it," and looking somewhere else for what I need in group life. It isn't here.

Irresponsibility and the wish to escape is present in many members of small group meetings in our churches. Sometimes they quit, never facing their own responsibility for the situation.

Mere physical membership in a group can change to an attitude of servantship, which includes a sense of responsibility for the welfare of the group. Consider the following quotation from the last meeting of a small group in which many of the members had made this kind of movement from irresponsibility to responsibility.

The character of the sessions has changed almost completely. There is no longer the fight to see who can talk the most or get their idea started. Now everyone has a responsible attitude and there is a sense of caring that has only been fleeting heretofore. Of course the tendency is to say why couldn't we have done this long ago. However, I realize, as I have in the back of my mind all the time, that all the pain and agony had to be suffered to get to this point of open creative action.

There have been personality alterations here which I would have insisted at the beginning could never have happened. I hoped that I could someway be opened up but really sort of felt in the back of my mind that this group would just be like many others. It was not like other groups, though. There has been a change in my outlook. I was finally forced to look at myself as acutely as I have looked at others, and I found that if things are going to change that I would have to take more responsibility than I have been taking. When I saw that another member could make such a change, I was encouraged to make the attempt for myself. It felt as if a great weight were lifted, and having to speak about myself tonight was a pleasant experience instead of the frightening one it would have been.

4. *A movement from secrecy to sharing.* There are various ways to describe this secrecy. In the first session George Stevens expressed the hope that "I can overcome this habit of keeping a defensive wall up and trap shut during the first and even subsequent group encounters." Members remain hidden and silent. Often such secrecy stems from a defensiveness and a fear of rejection. It is safer to remain hidden than to risk a negative evaluation by the group, or even outright rejection. In the first session George revealed all of these feelings—feelings of rejection, defensiveness, hostility, and fear of evaluation. He wrote, "I am reacting in the same old way; my anger shuts me up; I just don't talk when I'm mad." Then another member tried to interpret and to evaluate George's contribution as mere "intellectualism." Angry and defensive, George was unable to respond. He took it as a rejection. In this mood he remained hidden, although he wished that he could share all of what he was feeling.

It is instructive to note here that we often interpret silence as secrecy and talking as sharing. It is true that a member must eventually talk in order to share, but talking can be a way of remaining hidden too. Talk can be participation on a superficial level. By talking endlessly about some questions, those which are more acceptable and safe, the meeting can keep the real questions, which are touchy and difficult, hidden. George Stevens put this very well in his final paragraph where he indicated something of his movement from secrecy to sharing as well as to a more mature way of understanding his own silence or participation.

> I guess the greatest realization [for me] is the fact that when one goes into a group with the intense feeling that he must talk and then he doesn't, he is pushing authenticity out the window if he forces himself to talk. For me—I realize that when I have something to say, I can and will say it. This is a movement from "nervous duty" to a comfortable desire to be a part of what is going on *either* silently *or* verbally.

A church member once phrased the issue in this fashion, "If I can't be myself here in the church, where else can I go?" This member had discovered that the life he was living required a good deal of secrecy. It was safer that way. Yet he longed for a place where he could be known and where he could be open. He had heard the message of the church correctly. It is to be a community where we are known before God and our fellowmen. The problem for many members today is that even the church in its meetings encourages secrecy rather than sharing.

5. *A movement from unfreedom to freedom.* In the initial meetings it is quite clear that George Stevens was struggling to become free from a number of things. One might describe it as inhibition, but it is more than that; it is a lack of freedom, or what we have called "unfreedom." George was struggling to become free from his sense of inadequacy, free from his frustrating need to keep up a defensive wall and maintain a silence, free from his old bondage to anger which shut him up, free from his feelings of alienation from others (especially strangers), free from his frightened "shutupness" that kept him from making the witness he wished to make at a given time, and free from doing anything—such as talking—as a "nervous duty." In all of these struggles with "unfreedom," George was asking a question that remains largely unspoken in our churches: "Can I be myself, my own good and bad self, and be accepted by this church

group or by the church fellowship? Or, do I have to be something I ain't (to put it in the vernacular) in order to belong here?"

By the end of the meetings, George had achieved a measure of freedom in all of these areas. Now he felt that he could talk not only from "nervous duty" but also on the basis of a genuine authenticity. He could accept either his silence or his speaking. In the seventh meeting he wrote, "It was really a good feeling to realize that I had opened myself to the group." Alongside this growing sense of freedom, we find a growing sense of responsibility. The member is truly free only as he is also responsible.

Another way in which to interpret this movement from unfreedom to freedom is to consider the member's reaction to authority. Many authorities are present in every meeting. The leader, the group, other members, the purpose of the meeting, and the rules for the meeting may be authorities for the members. The two classic responses to authority are conformity (submission) or rebellion (hostility). But neither conformity nor rebellion gives a member genuine freedom for his life in the group. These reactions stifle each individual's unique and creative response. Conformity and rebellion cannot be our only reaction to authority, though they may be necessary on occasion. We cannot escape the various authorities in our lives, but we can moderate our responses to authority. The movement from unfreedom to freedom is characterized by the increase of a third reaction to authority; namely, responsible participation. There is a growing sense of freedom. The relationship to authority enables the member to become that which God intended.

George Stevens began to show some freedom for himself by a sense of adequacy, confidence, and courage to face not only personal problems but also future group encounters. He began to show a reaction to the authority of the group but moved on to a sense of responsible participation on behalf of himself and others.

6. *A movement from mistrust to trust.* A sense of trust-worthiness about one's self and a reasonable trustfulness in relation to others is a primary ingredient of a healthy personality. Trust or its opposite (mistrust) is the primary learning of the infant. This is a learning that goes on throughout life; adults struggle with trust and mistrust too. We see the struggle in George Stevens. In the opening sessions he was expressing some mistrust by his tendency to withdraw into himself. Increasingly, however, he began to feel that he could trust this small group meeting. By the tenth meeting he was able to say, "The group feels like an old shoe, comfortable and nice."

Movement by a member from mistrust to trust is a recurrent theme in many personal reflections about our life together in meetings. You often find phrases such as, "I still find it difficult to put full trust in anyone—my trust has been misused." Yet as we saw in a previous chapter, the ability to trust is one of the deepest religious dimensions. We are talking about our faith when we talk about our trust in God and our trust in our neighbor. It is of crucial importance that the group demonstrate its trustworthiness because only as trust is experienced will the members, caught in a web of mistrust, be able to trust. A member once suggested the "chicken and egg" nature of this issue by recognizing that "a member wants the group to prove itself trustworthy before he will trust it, and the reverse must be true: only if some of us have the guts to trust the group with our inner lives will the group be able to become trustworthy." Another member once described his experience in a meeting in the following way:

> Specifically, the release for me in the group came when I realized (as I now see) that we didn't talk about basic Christian trust, but the group trusted me and the immediate trust is real. I feel some shame that I monopolized the group with such a personal problem. But it was for me an existential ex-

perience of actually "seeing" how both content and process constitute the Christian community or group.

This movement might be characterized as a change from a sense of strangeness to a sense of at-homeness. Moving from mistrust to trust means that the member now feels he belongs. Everyone wants to belong to a group that is trustworthy. Persons seek a community that will redeem them, to which they can belong fully and in which they will be known. When this sense of trust comes upon the members of a meeting, one is reminded in a powerful way of Ephesians 2:19-22:

> So then you are no longer strangers and sojourners, but you are fellow citizens with the saints and members of the household of God, built upon the foundation of the apostles and prophets, Christ Jesus himself being the cornerstone, in whom the whole structure is joined together and grows into a holy temple in the Lord; in whom you also are built into it for a dwelling place of God in the Spirit.

7. *A movement from the need to receive ministry to a concern to give ministry.* No member ever completely outgrows the need for help, but the mature member who has become a servant of the group has what one might call an "excess" of love. He is free to act out this love in ministry to his fellows. We move back and forth, sometimes giving, sometimes receiving help. A person cannot bear his burden alone.

The member who is becoming a servant often needs ministry himself in the beginning. He says, "How can I possibly help anyone else when I have not been helped myself?" In many ways George Stevens was expressing this feeling through the first several meetings. He was searching for help. He hardly thought about giving help; he was so concerned about finding help for himself. In the seventh meeting he found it, "I really don't know what induced me to speak but perhaps it was the feeling that this group was open and accepting. I was moved by Art's honesty the week before and the way the group worked with him. This was the help I guess I was looking for. It was a really good feeling to realize that I had opened myself to the group." From this beginning we see movement culminating in the eleventh meeting where he wrestled with the problem of how he could minister to Robert. He had received ministry; he wanted to minister to others.

8. *A movement from a closed mind to a mind open to learning.* Educators as well as churchmen are puzzled as to how and when persons are prepared to learn. There is no end to the knowledge which is offered to us, but many of us are incapable of accepting this knowledge. We are not open to learning.

In the beginning, the diary of George Stevens reveals that he was quite closed to new knowledge because of his feelings of isolation, anxiety, and defensiveness—all of which contributed to a closed mind. The diary entry for the fifth meeting has a reference to this whole issue. George had said something about his lack of openness. He thought that people were trying to lead him to knowledge but that they could not force him to accept it because he was not ready. However John interpreted this statement as just another "intellectualism" without any real meaning for George. John labeled it with the old saw, "You can lead me to the water, but you can't make me drink." George was too angry to respond, but his diary shows that his comment was a genuine effort on his part to communicate with the group about his personal condition and need; namely, "I am anxious and my mind is still closed even though there is much to learn here."

Some movement is apparent by the end of the meetings. The last entry in the diary, particularly the questions, shows that George Stevens was now prepared to listen to some answers. He was asking some questions. How does one learn about himself? Does the individual have to grow in personal insight? What can we do for another member? He revealed a genuine openness of mind, now self-directed and self-motivated. He wanted to learn. Learning now would make a difference. Facing a genuine problem, he felt a need for knowledge. Thus George no longer felt so personally threatened that he could not look around him and entertain new knowledge and new ideas. The threat to himself had diminished.

It may well be that we resist knowledge, resist new ideas, resist being communicated with more than we have ever realized. Maybe we are afraid of that invasion of the self which listening and accepting involves. Maybe people are scared to death of a new idea. Sometimes it frightens them. Personal growth is difficult, if not impossible, without this movement from a closed mind to an open mind.

Productive work is very difficult under intense emotional tension. It is clear in George Stevens' diary that his productive learning and knowledge-seeking was low in the beginning of the meetings when his personal tension was high. The possibilities of his learning became greater as the tension decreased in the latter sessions. It is true that George Stevens had learned something about himself. What he had learned allowed him to open himself to further learning. Have you noticed how a conference or workshop always takes several days to get down to productive work? The emotional tensions have to be cleared away before the members can really give themselves to the task at hand.

9. *A movement from fear of self, neighbor, and God to love of self, neighbor, and God.* The most valuable learning for a member and the learning that most characterizes the servant is an increase in the love of God, neighbor, and self. This is the fundamental task of the church. God, neighbor, and self are interrelated; if you increase the love in any one

of the three relationships, you affect the other relationships. We can look at any one of the relationships for evidence of growth in the others. The diary of George Stevens affords us evidence of this growth. He became more capable of loving and accepting himself, and he certainly became more able to love his neighbor, especially Robert, about whom he was so concerned. The frustrations of the fifth meeting diminished in subsequent sessions. We have evidence of the movement from a fear of self and neighbor (and also, God) to an increase of the love of God, neighbor, and self.

The interrelationship between feelings for self, neighbor, and God often occurs. For example, a theological student talking to his pastor said, "I don't care about myself, I don't think—I don't like myself. Therefore if I hate myself, I don't express myself to anyone else." And again, "It's awfully hard to try and show a love to my parents when I don't care very much about myself, and I don't dare let out too much or else Mom gets worried . . . you know, it's strange how a person can get himself so tied up with this until he becomes almost evil. That's when you start hating yourself, and you're not giving anyone else a break either."

Some weeks later after further conversations with his pastor, this person had changed his attitude toward self, neighbor, and God. Here are his words:

> I get to thinking about the patience that God has with people. It amazes me. . . . When it comes down to it, I've got more faith than I realize. Sure a lot of specifics never turned out because I guess they couldn't turn out. God isn't going to work with what isn't; we are people, we are free to come and go as we choose and we've got ourselves all bottled up with anxieties, frustrations, and hatreds. I guess God isn't going to make us puppets by turning us into something, because that isn't the way he works. But the amazing thing is that in spite of it all, I've never been let down.
>
> If God was something domineering (this idea just popped into my mind) who treated us like a puppet on a string, what

respect would we have for him? We hate domineering parents, employers, and things like that . . . but in spite of it all, he has always been faithful to me.

My rebirth is going to be one of those slow steady things; growing in grace—why, when the apostle Paul had that experience, he suddenly came to a realization of his guilt and went off to meditate for three years. I might say I had the same kind of experience recently. I am beginning to get a deeper understanding of what Paul was saying. It is a personal testimony of his own, "It is no longer I who live, but Christ who lives in me."

To be crucified with Christ is suddenly to be freed, to be released from the sin that plagued you before, to the freedom that you suddenly feel as a result of your union with Christ. To me I think my growth as a person and my regaining self-appreciation is going to be a religious experience as well as something strictly personal.

I suddenly begin to feel that I am downright satisfied. Let life bring what it will. It has taken a while for me to accept myself, my limitations, my fears, my hatreds, my misunderstandings, but I am getting gradually to the place where I can look at most of them objectively and say, "Now this is what I've got to work with." And, I believe, unconsciously I am, because all of this hasn't been downright conscious development either. It has been surprising. I'm beginning to break through this doggone shell.

From a fear or hatred of self, neighbor, and God, this person moved to a love for self, neighbor, and God. This most fundamental movement of all transforms a member into a servant of the Lord Jesus Christ.

Very soon you will be attending another meeting. You may be hopeful or discouraged about the prospect. If you want the meeting to be different in any way, the only person you can really change is yourself. Others may respond to your initiative, but blaming others is not very helpful and prodding others to change is not very successful. Change begins with you.

APPENDIX

QUESTIONS OFTEN ASKED ABOUT THE VIEWPOINT PRESENTED IN THIS BOOK

1. *How can I start a group that will take its life together seriously, as suggested in this book?*

You can start a new group by talking to the people you know, asking them if they are interested in a different kind of group—one that takes seriously not only the discussion but also the dynamics of the meeting. Ask them to join you in the experiment. New groups might be organized around many different areas of interest: parents of an age group, church school teachers, church officers, a study group.

You can start more slowly by adding a third member to a significant conversation you have with one person. Keep adding members as they indicate a serious interest.

Start a group in any way that is comfortable for you. Make it clear that the group is going to talk about "how they are doing" as well as a particular topic. Once evaluation is experienced, each group will begin to organize itself in a meaningful way. The meetings will probably develop in ways you had not expected.

2. *What about the regular groups of the church—deacons, trustees, church school classes, women's circles—don't they have too much business to spend time in evaluation?*

The business of the church is much more than the maintenance of the organization. To continue to do the business without considering the dynamics of the meeting, shortchanges the members. To continue to ignore process and responsibility and evaluation is to continue with meetings that are not as rewarding as they can be. Existing groups can profit immensely by evaluation. Strengthen the existing boards, classes, and committees of the church by an examination of how they are functioning. Many people have found that evaluation has helped accomplish the business more efficiently and has greatly increased the rewards for the members.

3. *What if the minister isn't interested?* (A layman)

Are you sure? Have you talked with him, sharing the ideas of this book and your own convictions about the meetings in your church? If you have made every effort and he has not been enthusiastic, you can still begin in the groups for which you are responsible and in which you are a member. Increase your helpfulness to the group.

4. *What if the lay people are not interested?* (A minister)

Are you sure? Have you tried evaluation, for example, in several groups? Don't just talk about doing it. Do it. Persons are hesitant about new things they have not experienced.

Start new groups by getting people together who have similar concerns—grief, vocational decision, marital conflict—and practice evaluation and the ideas of this book from the beginning. Have all members read the book as their entry requirement.

5. *What can you do about a person who always dominates the group?*

Sooner or later during the evaluation, the members of the group will help such a person see what he is doing to the group. The use of the checklist invariably raises the issue of domination. Often dominating members begin to recognize themselves when they check the list. The ensuing discussion brings it out in the open.

If the group has no established time or procedures for evaluation, the members must have the courage to call attention to what is happening to the group. If you feel dominated, then somehow, with as much courtesy as you can muster, you must share your honest feelings with the group and with the person who is doing the dominating, whether he be minister, elder statesman, or newcomer.

6. *What should be done about silent members?*

Let them alone. If the group is so talkative that there is no silent time when a quiet person can speak, then the group ought to mend its ways. Otherwise, silent members will speak when ready; efforts to get them to say something by asking them questions only frighten them.

7. *What material should we study?*

The group ought to make this decision. If a leader or a part of the group decides, the other members may be reluctant participants. The particular study material chosen does not affect the concern with the relationships in the meeting.

8. *Should a group take in new members?*

The introduction of new members always changes a group. If an intensive kind of experience has been achieved, new members threaten this relationship and the new member himself is uneasy. On the other hand, many groups must take in new members. New members should be briefed by the total group and brought up-to-date on how the group functions.

9. *What can you do about conflict in a group?*

Conflict should be acknowledged and dealt with. It produces a potentially creative time. To ignore conflict is not to eliminate it. Conflict will remain smoldering under the surface. Deal with it.

Defensive, hostile, angry feelings should be faced as well.

10. *How long does this evaluation have to go on?*

Evaluation is one method for accomplishing a life style in a group. That style is one of openness and of facing problems. Examination of the group's life together becomes a permanent part of the meetings, not just a sometime thing.

11. *Isn't there a shortcut? All of this will take too much time.*

I know of no shortcut to improved group relationships. In the long run, paying attention to how the meeting functions may save a great deal of time. Members will be enabled and encouraged to share all of their resources and to share responsibility for the meeting.

If this book is the common property of all members of a group, the opportunity to improve the group's functioning will be readily available. The time taken in the beginning will save time in the end, with the additional benefit of more rewarding experiences for the members.

12. *Isn't this just group psychotherapy?*

Yes and no. Psychotherapy means soul healing, which has been the church's business for centuries. Proposed here are ways and means for making the many meetings in the church matter more for their members. If some of the proposals are similar to methods used by professional group psychotherapists, that fact should not bar our use of them. The concern and methods of this book grow out of the fundamental purpose of the church to increase the love of God and the love of neighbor.

NOTES

1. Richard Baxter, *The Reformed Pastor* (Richmond, Va.: John Knox Press, 1963).

2. H. Richard Niebuhr *et al.*, *The Purpose of the Church and Its Ministry* (New York: Harper & Bros., 1956), p. 31.

3. Carl R. Rogers, *On Becoming a Person* (Boston: Houghton Mifflin Co., 1961), p. 332.

4. Erik H. Erikson, "Identity and the Life Cycle," *Psychological Issues*, I, 1, chap. ii.

5. Paper presented by William Glasser, M.D., Brentwood San Vincenta Medical Center, Los Angeles, California, at the 32d Annual Governors' Conference on Youth, in Chicago, Illinois, May 10, 1963.

6. Martin Luther, "A Treatise on Christian Liberty" in *Three Treatises* (Philadelphia: Fortress Press, 1943), pp. 251-290.

7. Paul Tillich, *The Protestant Era* (Chicago: University of Chicago Press, 1948), chap. xi.

8. Hendrik Kraemer, *A Theology of the Laity* (Philadelphia: Westminster Press, 1958), p. 187. © Hendrik Kraemer.

FOR FURTHER READING

Brunner, H. Emil. *The Misunderstanding of the Church*. Philadelphia: Westminster Press, 1953. A classic theological and historical examination demonstrating that the church must be both a fellowship and an institution.

Egan, Gerard. *Face to Face*. Monterey, CA: Brooks/Cole Publishing Co., 1973. A very readable introduction to the small-group experience and interpersonal growth.

Fox, Matthew. *Original Blessing*. Santa Fe: Bear & Co., 1983. Not specifically about meetings. The author compares Fall/Redemption and Creation-centered Spirituality. The latter lifts up an exciting new way of thinking about spirituality, creation, letting go, pain, salvation, compassion, celebration, and justice. Useful for theological reflection about our life together.

Greenleaf, Robert K. *Servant Leadership*. New York: Paulist Press, 1977. Develops the thesis that servant and leader can be fused in one real person at all levels of status and calling. Chapters on many of our institutions including the church.

Johnson, David W. and Frank P. *Joining Together*. Englewood Cliffs, NJ, 1975. A large volume for training about group theory and group skills with many exercises included.

Jourard, Sidney M. *The Transparent Self*. Rev. ed., New York: Van Nostrand, 1971. A series of essays about the power of self-disclosure to enable persons to change.

111

Leas, Speed. *Leadership and Conflict*. Nashville: Abingdon Press, 1982. Addressed to those who have leadership skills and responsibilities. Deals with our fear of conflict and has specific helps for certain conflict situations.

Miller, Sherod; Elam W. Nunnally; and Daniel B. Wackman. *Alive and Aware*. Minneapolis: Interpersonal Communications Programs, Inc. 1975. All about improving your relationships through effective communication. There are exercises and theory applicable to daily living and group life.

Niebuhr, H. Richard, et al. *The Purpose of the Church and Its Ministry*. New York: Harper and Bros., 1961. A biblical and theological statement on the task of the church which has become a classic.

Nouwen, Henri J.M. *Reaching Out: The Three Movements of the Spiritual Life*. Garden City, NY: Doubleday & Co., 1975. The second movement, from hostility to hospitality, is especially relevant for church meetings.

Satir, Virginia. *Making Contact*. Millbrae, CA: Celestial Arts, 1976. Elaborates on the postscript theme of contact. Change in perception brings about change in action.

Satir, Virginia. *Peoplemaking*. Palo Alto, CA: Science and Behavior Books, Inc., 1972. Very readable and usable exposition about self-worth. How each person feels about himself or herself affects the way we participate in our families, our work, and our church meetings.

Worley, Robert C. *A Gathering of Strangers: Understanding the Life of Your Church*. Philadelphia: Westminster Press, 1976. Ideas and tools to enable a congregation to become a people united in mission and more truly the "body of Christ" performing Christ's ministry.

POSTSCRIPT 1987

This postscript expands on the communication process described in chapter III as "expression, listening, and response." The important new word is CONTACT. As we communicate with one another in the group, what kind of contact are we making? Contact is our experience of the other person taken in through one of our five senses: hearing, seeing, touching, tasting, and smelling. We know when we have been contacted by touch. We are "in touch." We feel it on our bodies. Contact by words and hearing is more difficult. And the contact we can make through our eyes is often overlooked. Taste and smell will not be considered here, although memory of important events in life is often more powerfully stirred by smell than by any other sense.

What kind of contact are we making with one another in our meetings through our talking, listening, looking, and touching? Is the contact with others sharp or dull, understandable or confusing, clear or obtuse? Good contact is to see, hear, and feel what is going on right now in the meeting. Poor contact is to deflect, shy away from, be afraid of what we are experiencing now. In the midst of the meeting you and I can take responsibility for the kind of contact we are making. Here are some of the things we can do. We cannot change others. We *can* change our own ways of making contact.

The Deacons' meeting was discussing the previous Sunday's

communion service. Fred said, looking at the wall above the faces across from him, "We didn't like the service." The minister felt his stress level rise. The chairman was embarrassed and looked at his notes. Someone commented on the flower arrangement. The members were making poor contact with one another.

Fred made his statement again. This time the person sitting next to him reached out and touched his forearm, turned, looked him in the eyes, and in a gentle voice said, "I appreciated the service. For whom are you speaking, Fred?" After further discussion, Fred agreed that he was speaking only for himself. He had not checked out his perception with anyone else. "I didn't like the service." He went on to say what had bothered him and how he would like to see the service conducted. Others expressed their feelings and hopes. The members were making good contact with one another. Let us examine the several dimensions of contact in this illustration.

MAKING CONTACT WITH OUR TALKING

The words we choose can increase or decrease the contact we make with the other members of the group. Here are several questions about the implications of the language we use.

1. Am I choosing "I" and taking responsibility for my statements? You and I think we are being polite by saying "we, you, it, one," etc. when we really mean "I." We do not know what others are thinking. We assume and imagine what others feel, without checking it out with them. Contact will increase as we own our feelings and ideas in the meeting. Inappropriate pronouns increase generalizations, abstractions, and discussions that are unfocused and rambling.

2. Am I choosing verbs that sharpen contact with others by indicating my responsibility in the situation? Fred might have said, "I can't tell you what kind of service I need." "Can't" implies that forces over which we have no control are preventing us from speaking or acting. A more honest statement

would be "I won't." The group can accept this decision and offer to help Fred share what is preventing him from telling the group what he wants. Fred's willingness to share will depend on the trust level in the group.

Other verbs to watch are *have to* as opposed to *choose to*, *need* as opposed to *want*, and *know* as opposed to *assume* or *imagine*. I "have to" go to church implies a demand; "I choose to" go to church is a stronger statement and better contact. "I need" your help implies necessity. There are few necessities. "I want your help" gives the other person a choice. "I know" when I don't really know is to prejudge what others are thinking and feeling.

Contact can be strengthened by our choice of verbs.

3. Am I asking a question when making my own statement would be much sharper and faster contact with the others? The person responding to Fred first made a statement and then asked for clarification of "we." Many questions put responsibility on the others, when the speaker really wants to make his or her own statement. If a pastor asks, "What did you think about the annual meeting?" members of the meeting may be thrown into an unnecessary guessing dilemma. Does he really want to know? I wonder what she thinks. Is there room for criticism? If the pastor makes a straight statement of where she stands, "I liked the annual meeting with the exception of the too long discussion about cleaning the building," the members are free to go ahead with their own statements. The speaker has risked himself or herself. Contact is poorer when members have to mind read what someone else is really thinking and feeling, when they are put on the spot by a question.

"Why" questions often lead to an endless chain of "why" questions. Answers will be as varied as the number of persons present. "What" and "how" questions usually lead to specificity and not endless explanations. How could the communion service be strengthened? What changes can we plan for our next service?

4. Am I saying where I stand on an issue? Are my "yes" and my "no" clear, or am I hedging with qualifiers like maybe, try, possibly, leaving the contact muddy? "Maybe I'll come." "I might possibly do that." One of the most misused words is "try." Try to pick up a pencil! Either you do or you don't pick up the pencil.

5. Am I neutralizing contact by "yes, but" and "if only" sentences? "That was a good sermon last Sunday, Pastor, but I did not like the way you ended it." The pastor forgets the affirmation as he or she struggles to remember the ending. "I would come to your meeting if only there was a different leader/a different subject." "If only" disguises the ways we want others to be different before we will join. We can only control ourselves, not others.

6. Am I repeating myself, unnecessarily illustrating my point, inappropriately referring to the past or to the future, rather than staying with the here and now? Contact is decreased when we go beyond the words that make our point.

7. Am I "lecturing" to others with "shoulds" and "oughts," rather than talking about what "is" and how I feel and think about the issue? Judgment often decreases contact. People stop listening. In contrast, words of appreciation to the persons around me in the meeting often increase contact.

MAKING CONTACT WITH OUR LISTENING

Listening (see pp. 28ff.) is a means of increasing or decreasing the contact we are making with other people. When we pay attention to the speaker and "really hear" the other, the contact is exciting and enlivening. Our preoccupation with what we want in the meeting gets in the way of hearing. We cannot pay attention to two or three things at once. Two questions will focus the issue.

1. Am I hearing what's going on, or is my mind preoccupied with the past or the future or what I will say next? To be in touch with another person through hearing the words the person is saying takes effort and desire to come into

contact with that person. To let go of our own agenda and give up for this moment our own preoccupations, so we can *hear* the other, is finally a gift both to the other and to ourselves. When I am able to hear in this manner, I am always surprised at the contact I make with the person. Truly hearing the story of a life is endlessly fascinating. Meetings are enriched by contactful listening.

2. Am I assuming that I know what others think, feel, and experience? I do not really need to listen. Or I can half listen because I can imagine what someone else is thinking. Such listening is poor contact and belittles the other. I need to hear and check out with the other person in order to "know" and fully to contact him or her.

MAKING CONTACT WITH OUR LOOKING

You and I have been in meetings where a member looks at everything and everybody except the person to whom she or he is speaking. Much of the possible contact of the speaker's words is lost as she or he looks at the rug, out the window, or at a spot three feet above your head. You and I can choose to look directly at the person to whom we are speaking. When a person looks directly at us while speaking we are doubly contacted, through our hearing and our sight.

We can ask another person to look directly at us or at the person being addressed. If the person hesitates or objects, we can ask, "What do you think will happen if you look at the person as you speak?" The answer may surprise us. "I'm unsure of myself." "I'm afraid." "I don't think she would like that." In which case we can check that out with her.

People know the power of eye contact. Salespersons learn to do it. Why not Christians? Contact with our looking builds the relationship we crave. We want to be seen by our neighbor. It is one of the ways that we know we belong and that we feel loved. We want to see our neighbor. Giving persons the permission to look at each person around the group, making eye contact, sometimes yields unexpected benefits. After this simple "looking" exercise let them comment about what happened to them.

No person wants to be "overlooked." We spend years together as members of the same church and sitting in the same meetings. Yet if we are asked to describe our friend's face from memory, we may hesitate. Before reading on, describe the face of one of your church friends. Chances are that even after all these meetings we forgot the color of the eyes, or the jut of the chin or a birthmark. We have never really seen our neighbor or been seen by our neighbor. Is the looking contact among the members in your meetings good or indifferent or poor?

The eyes have been called "the windows of the soul." Visual contact can be misused and can be inappropriate in some places and at some times. Is not church, however, a place to let our souls be seen?

MAKING CONTACT WITH OUR TOUCHING

Newborn babies will wither, and even die, without touch. Touching and being touched continue to be important contacts whereby we know in a significant nonverbal way that we belong and that we are loved. During the civil rights struggles in the South in the sixties, observers were puzzled about the stamina and strength of black children subjected to jeers and isolation as schools were slowly integrated. No fancy psychiatric or sociological theory seemed to fit. Almost by accident the observers discovered that when a frightened black child went home after school each day, her mother would hold her, they would touch each other, and through repeated physical contact, the fear was lessened and strength regained for the next day.

The Gospels are filled with references to touching: healing experiences, anointing for honoring and healing, the holy kiss, footwashing, the laying on of hands, and the references where Jesus made contact by touching persons. Through the centuries the church has practiced some of these touch contacts. In our own generation we are slowly recovering the permission and freedom to touch again. How necessary in a culture where it often appears that touch is only for violence or for sex. In a high-tech society we need high-touch more than ever. There is a touch hunger in our society and the church has an ancient mandate to make physical contact available among its members, in church, nursing home, hospital, and meeting.

Church members have responded. In recent years there has been a growing freedom to hug one another, to express care with a hand on a shoulder, to hold a hand in the hospital, to join hands in prayer, and to find touching experiences beyond the perfunctory handshake. Verbal and visual contacts alone leave one feeling isolated from one's own body and from other persons.

There are important personal boundaries to be observed as church members begin to explore contact with touch. Child abuse, molestation, battered women, sexual implications can be tragic misuses of bodily contact. Such abuse, however, may be the result of the absence of contact by touch in the lives of persons. Each church meeting will find its own appropriate level of touch contact. When Fred's arm was touched in the Deacons' meeting, communication and caring were immediately increased. We are embodied persons. And God created our bodies and found them good. Church meetings will matter more and be more healing and wholistic when we become comfortable in making contact with our touching.

Church meetings still matter.

EVALUATING THE CONTACT I AM MAKING IN THE MEETING*

The only person we can change is ourself. Changing our own behavior may have an effect on others. If we make good contact, others are likely to respond in kind. This checklist can be used in the evaluation time of the meeting (see pp. 53ff.) or discussed with one other person or used for personal reflection.

	Always	Usually	Occasionally	Seldom	Never	Excessively
MAKING CONTACT WITH MY TALKING						
1. I say "I" and not "you, we, one," when I speak for myself						
2. I choose verbs of responsibility—won't, want, choose to						
3. I make statements and do not ask questions to shift responsibility						
4. I state where I stand without qualifiers—"try, maybe, possibly,"						
5. I eliminate "yes, but" and "if only" sentences						
6. I stop when my point is made and do not repeat and ramble						
7. I accept others, and let go of my judgments and do not lecture						
8. I express appreciation						
MAKING CONTACT WITH MY LISTENING						
9. I hear the others and do not assume that I know what they think and feel						
MAKING CONTACT WITH MY LOOKING						
10. I look people in the eye as I speak to them						
MAKING CONTACT WITH MY TOUCHING						
11. I appropriately touch others						